BOULDER COUNTY BEER

A Refreshing History

Michael J. Casey

AMERICAN PALATE

Published by American Palate
A Division of The History Press
Charleston, SC
www.historypress.com

Front cover: Flatirons overlooking Boulder Valley. *Author photo.*

First published 2021

Manufactured in the United States

ISBN 9781467144759

Library of Congress Control Number: 2020945741

Notice: The information in this book is true and complete to the best of our knowledge. It is offered without guarantee on the part of the author or The History Press. The author and The History Press disclaim all liability in connection with the use of this book.

For Lindsay

CONTENTS

AN INTRODUCTION BY WAY OF ACKNOWLEDGEMENT

No work exists in a vacuum, and no writer works alone. An entire support staff is required to print one word, and a convergence of seemingly random events and players must work in harmony before those words even form. And to that aim, let's begin at the beginning.

My career in beer grew out of necessity. I had been reviewing movies for a local newspaper, *Boulder Weekly*, for a little over two years when my editor, Amanda Moutinho, called me over to Southern Sun Pub & Brewery for a meeting. Located across the street from the *Boulder Weekly* office, Southern Sun functions as the editorial staff's second conference room. Amanda and I occasionally met there to discuss movies we had seen and plan future coverage, but that day she had other motives.

"We need a beer writer," she said. "And Joel [Dyer, the paper's editor] knows you like to drink."

Not one to turn down more column space, I responded enthusiastically but countered: How about a column on wine? I liked beer and drank plenty of it, but I knew next to nothing about the beverage beyond that. Wine, on the other hand, I had sold, tasted and studied. I had hosted food and wine pairing seminars and led tours of a winery. Grapes were in my wheelhouse, and working up articles about best buys, coverage of that year's crop and suggestions of what to drink with what you eat wouldn't be difficult.

"Sounds interesting," she responded. "But, we need a beer column."

So, I began writing about beer.

I started by touring each brewery in Boulder County, one each week, and writing about what I found and drank. Along the way, I perused the pages of periodicals like *Craft Beer & Brewing*, the *New Brewer* and *Zymurgy*. My sister and her husband gifted me with Jeff Alworth's *The Beer Bible* (my most consulted resource), and just as one beer led to another, Alworth's *Bible* led to full shelves of literature on beer and the history of brewing. The more I read, the more my writing changed from a man-about-town column into something more interested in specific beer styles, the history of brewing and interviews with local brewers.

But with each beer, book and interview, I grew less and less confident in my estimation about beer, how much I understood about it and why Boulder County ended up as *the* place for the craft beer revolution. I started seeking concrete answers to fill the gaps left in other literature. Only, each time I found one, another ten questions popped up. But the beauty of being a columnist is that no one article need encapsulate everything. There's always next week, and if not for the editorial staff of *Boulder Weekly*—Emma Athena, Matt Cortina, Joel Dyer, Angela K. Evans, Josh Gross, Amanda Moutinho and Caitlin Rockett—I would not have had the space and freedom to work through these (sometimes conflicting) thoughts and observations. And with that, I extend my thanks to Susan France, *Boulder Weekly*'s resident photographer and director of production, founder/CEO Stewart Sallo and publisher Francis Zankowski.

Here's the part where I thank those who had a hand in this journey. First, the brewers—they shared their stories, and they shared their beers. Those who directly contributed to this book are listed in the bibliography, but not mentioned are the number of public relations representatives who set up those interviews and tracked down long-forgotten photos: Tess McFadden and Sierra Koenig (Boulder Beer); Chad Melis (Oskar Blues); Jill Preston (Left Hand); Krista St. Charles, Vanessa Cory and Joe Osborne (Avery); and Megan Olson (New Belgium). Without their assistance, I—and every writer covering the beer scene—would be scrambling in the dark.

Speaking of those writers, I drew on many for this book, particularly Alicia Wallace's reporting at the *Boulder Daily Camera*; Ed Sealover, author of *Mountain Brew*; Dan Rabin, author of *Colorado Breweries*; Stephen Adams, chief operations officer of the website coloradobrewerylist.com; and Jonathan Shikes of *Westword* (more on him in a minute).

Equally important to piecing these stories together were the oral histories collected by Theresa McCulla of the Smithsonian Institute—they are all listed in the bibliography along with information about McCulla's Brewing

History Initiative—and the wealth of information and photos provided by the Brewers Association staff: Karna Murphy, Ann Obenchain and Luke Trautwein.

A few more: Scott Gerlach, who shared crucial homebrew information; Terri Takata-Smith of Downtown Boulder Partnership; and Sam Bock of History Center Colorado.

But before all those beautiful people got involved, *Boulder County Beer* was nothing more than a series of sketches and a few overarching thoughts on how brewery A connected to brewery B. And, like any writer uncertain of their material, I kept it to myself. Then a chance encounter with Shikes at the 2019 Big Beers, Belgians & Barleywines Festival in Breckenridge, Colorado, provided the catalyst.

Of all the beer festivals I've attended, Big Beers is my favorite. It is three days of seminars and tastings led by legacy and the up-and-coming brewers with a concluding commercial tasting of some of the best beers in the world. It was at the tasting that Shikes and I found each other in the same line.

We knew each other's bylines—at least I knew his—and we talked shop. I asked him what he was working on and expected a canned answer. He surprised me by answering honestly: a book about the history of brewing in Denver (titled *Denver Beer* and published by The History Press in spring 2020). We talked about the publisher and his approach for a few minutes, tried the beer we were waiting for and then went our separate ways.

In the adjoining room, my cutletsized consort was at the festival merchandise table, selecting sweaters for a friend—he was letting us use his condo for the weekend, and she wanted to leave him one as a good thank-you. I made my way through the crowd, found her, and with a mind flooded with beer, giddy from a day spent in seminars, I spoke these foolish words: "I think it's time to write a book."

"Lovely," she responded. "What do you think of this sweater?"

It was a nice sweater, and our friend loved it. And when I pitched the book to Artie Crisp at The History Press, he loved the idea too.

I DECIDED TO WRITE this book because I wanted to understand Boulder on a deeper level. Born and raised in the Denver suburb of Littleton—approximately forty miles south—the city of Boulder has always been a curiosity to me. My family and I would visit on occasion, my mother driving my sisters and me to see a Shakespeare play, to have afternoon tea at the Boulder Dushanbe Teahouse or to stick our feet in the icy cold creek that cuts through town. As an adult, I would return to the city sporadically, first to visit my sisters—both of whom graduated from the University of Colorado Boulder—and then regularly when I started working for the university and writing for the *Weekly*. That's when I started talking to brewers and discovered that almost all of them came from without: California, New Jersey, Chicago, New York City, the North, the South, even from overseas.

Why did they come here? Why did they choose Boulder? The choice seems almost arbitrary. Yet Boulder is home to the first craft brewery in Colorado and the first craft brewery east of the West Coast. It's the headquarters of the Brewers Association, the American Homebrewers Association and Brewers Publications. It's the birthplace of the Great American Beer Festival. And that's just the city. Open the iris up to include the full county, and you have at least three of the most significant breweries in the craft beer revolution, not to mention a slew of impressive, if not under-the-radar, breweries, brewpubs and taprooms.

But the two iconic beers of Colorado reside either south, in Golden, or north, in Fort Collins: Coors and Fat Tire, respectively. Just about every brewer interviewed in these pages had a chance encounter with a Fat Tire that changed their life. It's the beer that launched hundreds of Colorado breweries. If that's the case, why isn't Fort Collins the hub?

If there was an answer, I knew (hoped) it would present itself in print. The result is now in your hands.

The city of Boulder was once described as the "Athens of the Plains" and then as the "People's Republic of Boulder." It was once a haven for hippies and home to a football team that managed to sneak in a fifth down and win the game while time expired. It was also "dry." The country enacted Prohibition on January 17, 1920, but Colorado was ahead of the curve by four years. Boulder County outdid that by another seven, with the Better Boulder Party sweeping the Boulder City Council election of 1907. Teetotaler Isaac T. Earl was in as mayor, and intoxicating spirits were out.

But before that, Austrian-born William G. Cook came to Boulder by way of Illinois in 1863 and established the county's first brewery, Boulder City Brewery, as early as 1865. He started brewing on Pearl Street, between Broadway and Thirtieth Street, but proved to be an unsuccessful businessman. By 1874, the brewery was no more. A second Boulder City Brewery was erected at the intersection of Arapahoe Avenue and Lincoln Place. It lasted from 1875 to 1891, until it was sold and renamed the Boulder City Brewing Company. The name stuck until 1897, when new investors changed it again, this time to Crystal Springs Brewing & Ice Company. The brewery lasted until 1911—grandfathered in after the "dry" election of 1907.

"Shortly after the 1911 state elections, a new Colorado law banned billboard advertisement of liquor," wrote Robert W. McLeod in the book *Ghost Breweries of Colorado*. "The final entry in Boulder's city directory for Crystal Springs Brewery appeared that year. The brewery had finally been driven out of business five years before Colorado became a totally dry state."

Boulder would remain dry until 1967, when a large margin of Boulder voters, 71 percent, according to the *Daily Camera*, repealed Prohibition for good. A decade later, a couple of CU professors started conspiring about beer. We ought to start a brewery, one said to the other. The year is 1979, and Boulder County is home to zero breweries. That's all about to change.

PART I

BOULDER

1

GOAT SHED REVIVAL

"What are these hippies doing up here in Boulder?" Randolph Ware, cofounder of Boulder Brewing Company, chuckled while recalling the first time Bureau of Alcohol, Tobacco and Firearms (ATF) agent Lou Kravitzski visited Colorado's first craft brewery in the late 1970s.[1]

"He was not happy," Ware continued. "He had a gray suit and a thin, black acetate tie, and he was a big guy.

"At that time, the brewmaster was a guy by the name of Otto Zavatone," Ware said. "And Otto was a real character: storyteller, fisherman from Cape Cod, musician—he was the piano player in a band named the Fornicators." Ware also played in the Fornicators—saxophone. The two were housemates on a small farm where they raised and grew their own food.

Born on December 28, 1940, in Quincy, Massachusetts, Zavatone is one of those colorful characters who permeate the craft-brewing world. He played the B3 Hammond Organ on Del Shannon's "Runaway" and keyboard on Chuck Berry's "Johnny B. Goode." He shot guns with Hunter S. Thompson, worked as ski patrol at Aspen Highlands, was Boulder Brewing's first hire at Alvin Nelson's goat shed in Hygiene and was a raconteur of the highest accord.

"[Zavatone] and Lou go into the goat shed to show him what's going on, and they were in there about an hour," Ware continued. "When they came out, Lou was grinning from ear to ear. And the next time he showed up, [Lou] was on his Harley in his leathers.

Alvin Nelson's goats were equipped with bottle openers on their collars. Nelson demonstrates while Charlie Papazian looks on. *Courtesy Boulder Beer Co.*

"That was another one of those windows of things not being set up for success," Ware laughed.

Maybe it wasn't set up for success, but Boulder Brewing was too important to fail. A burgeoning industry was counting on it.

"Shoot, We Ought to Start a Brewery."

Like the greater craft beer revolution, Boulder's story begins in California, at a high school in South Pasadena, to be precise, where a skinny young Ware—or "Stick" as his older brother teased him—learned to homebrew from a friend's uncle, a ruffian on the lam from Louisiana and hiding out in California.

"He took [us] down to East L.A. and bought a bunch of brewing equipment," Ware said. "A crock, hydrometer and Blue Ribbon malt [an extract syrup that provides beer's fermentable sugars] and the rest and showed us how to make homebrew....We were using bread yeast and canned malt, and it was pretty hard to drink the stuff, but it was all we could get."

It was enough. Ware continued to brew up to and during his postdoctoral studies at the University of Colorado Boulder's Joint Institute for Laboratory

Astrophysics (JILA). There he crossed paths with the bald man with a thick Amish beard and no mustache: JILA chair David Hummer. And Hummer was homebrewing.

"He developed a method," Ware explained, "got some grain, some malted barley, and crushed them with a rolling pin." Hummer then added the crushed-up malt to a five-gallon thermos cooler, which he used as a makeshift mash tun.

"His wife was quite an accomplished artist and seamstress, and she made a filter out of a bridal veil that then went into the thermos cooler and kept the grains sequestered," Ware said. Hummer heated the water to about 170 degrees Fahrenheit, added it to the thermos, "stirred it up and let it sit for an hour, and then opened the little spout at the bottom.

"At first, it would come out as just mud," Ware said, "because of all the particles and everything else from the crushing. But then we would put it into a container of some kind and pour it back in the top, and after a short period of time, the husks from the malted barley would form their own filter.[2] It would become very bright. And then you could go ahead and put that into a crock and pitch the yeast in and start fermenting."

It was a world ahead of Ware's extract method, which limited the quality of the beer, by his admission.[3] "So, we started conspiring," Ware said.

David Hummer. *Courtesy Boulder Beer Co.*

DAVID HUMMER (1934–2016)

The eldest of four, David Graybill Hummer was born on November 4, 1934, in Lancaster County, Pennsylvania, into a Brethren family. "Anabaptist similar to the Amish and Mennonites," according to his son, Julius Hummer. "Significantly," Julius added, the family "didn't drink."

"In about 1960, he shipped out to England with a Fulbright to study physics at University College," Julius said. Hummer enjoyed London, from concerts to Indian food and typical pub ales: bitters, milds, pales and stouts—a far cry from standard American mass-marketed light lagers.

In 1961, Hummer received his PhD in astrophysics and met his wife, Janet Wood. A year later, Julius was born. And in 1965, the Hummers returned to the States, this time to Boulder, as David had a fellowship at CU's JILA. Around 1974, Hummer started homebrewing, according to Julius.

"The only packaged beer I ever remember being around the house were tallboy white steel cans of Country Club Malt Liquor," Julius recalled. "If this was the best he could buy, coming from London, he very likely did brew out of practical necessity.

"[Hummer] was an old-time liberal Democrat," Julius continued, pointing out that his father was "fiscally quite conservative" and believed money was to be saved, not spent.

"I remember one week before Christmas, he flew off to Duluth and bought the mill out of the Fitger's brewery," Julius said. "It was a good mill; it's still in use." The mill that Hummer recovered was for the newly constructed brewery on Wilderness Place. "I remember seeing the construction site before I left for brewing school in England in '84," Julius said. "Lo and behold, when I returned Christmas of '85, it was up and running."

But the 1980s were not easy for Hummer or the brewery. Between quality control issues, poorly designed and marketed beers and constant management changes, Hummer found himself more and more on the outside looking in. "I actually only remember David speaking bitterly about this one time," Julius said. "I know it hurt him. On the upside, by the time the second iteration [Rockies Brewing Company] had run its course, the folks at Boulder Beer Company were very good to my father and seemed to like involving him in their activities," Julius continued. "I remember him standing on a stage... saying, 'We started a revolution' to mass cheers."

David Hummer died at Boulder Community Health on December 17, 2016, following a brief illness. He was eighty-two.

Reflecting years later, Boulder Beer's director of sales, Dan Weitz, summed it up best: "They were making beer because they wanted to drink better beer."

And Hummer and Ware weren't alone. Friends, family and fellow faculty members all wanted to drink better beer—enough that it led Ware to an epiphany: "I just, off the top of my head, spouted, 'Shoot, we ought to start a brewery.'"

Let's back up. There is nothing unusual about saying, "We ought to start a brewery" in 2020, 2010 or 2000—even 1990, for that matter. But in the late 1970s, the notion of opening a brewery would have been on par with trying to start your own car company or manufacturing freeze-dried coffee.

Beer in the 1970s meant the big three, Anheuser-Busch, Coors and Miller; a few regionals, like Pabst Brewing Co. and Rainier Brewing Company; and two small breweries in California, Anchor Brewing in San Francisco and New Albion Brewing in Sonoma. Prohibition had wiped out the majority of American brewing, and those that remained were beginning to consolidate. Starting a brewery was simply not something one did.

"You know, my mom had always cautioned me against spouting off things, saying things, you weren't going to do," Ware said. "So, I kind of called myself on it."

Ware said Hummer would regularly claim, "I had talked him into doing the most irresponsible thing he'd ever done in his life, which was starting the brewery." Irresponsible or not, Ware and Hummer put their money where their mouths were. A fellow engineer at CU, Alvin Nelson, had a farm in Hygiene—north of Boulder and west of Longmont—they could use, and Ware and Hummer put together about $40,000 to get the operation rolling.

"You're Trying to Do What?"

Being first is never easy, especially when governmental red tape and paperwork are involved. "It was kind of, 'Oh, gee, we don't do things like that,'" Ware recounted.

But Ware kept calling down to Denver, getting passed around various departments and desks and making his way through the bureaucratic labyrinth that often waylays those with weaker constitutions until he got Harriett Bobo on the line. "And we hit it off," Ware said.

Born on October 10, 1942, in Florence, Alabama, Harriett Seretha Bobo is one of the unsung heroes in the craft beer movement. Her tenure with the ATF (then called the Alcohol and Tobacco Tax Division) began in New Orleans in 1965. Over the next thirty-seven years, Bobo worked her way up to senior executive service, working in Dallas, San Francisco, D.C. and, in the late 1970s, Denver, Colorado.

Bobo sent Ware the paperwork—more than Ware was expecting—and it sat on his kitchen table "for about six months," Ware said, "'cause it was about a foot deep."

But Bobo was there to help. "Don't be overwhelmed by it. I can help you out," she told him.

"She helped me through it. 'Fill this one out, do this one, do that one,'" Ware said. "Pretty soon, I had it done. And I talked to Hummer, and he said, 'Sure, let's see if we can get a license.'"

They submitted, and on September 25, 1979, Ware, Hummer and Nelson were issued the forty-third brewing license in America.

"THE EARLY CONSPIRACY."

Now they needed equipment. In Denver, they found an old stainless steel steam kettle for food preparation—thirty-five gallons by Ware's recollection. Raw materials came courtesy of Jeffrey Coors of the Coors Brewing Company. At the time, malt and hops were sold in bulk to breweries making millions of barrels of beer, not hundreds. Coincidentally, Coors's grandfather and Ware's grandmother had dated, and Coors thought it would be good to have a second Colorado brewery around for legislative purposes. Nelson's farm had a goat shed they could brew in, and Nelson, an adept engineer, could handle the plumbing. Zavatone would be the brewmaster.

"They told me I could be the brewmaster, except I had to build the brewery first!" Zavatone recounted in Charlie Papazian's *Microbrewed Adventures*.

"That was the early conspiracy," Ware said.

Their first beer brewed was a stout, and it won a blue ribbon at the American Homebrewers Association's first national competition.

"That kind of encouraged us," Ware said. Encouraging, yes, but the early years were still a lot of hard work. Thirty-five gallons at a time wasn't going to get the job done, and a goat shed wasn't the ideal place to brew.

American Homebrewers Association

On October 14, 1978, President Jimmy Carter changed the course of brewing history with the stroke of his pen. Though the Twenty-First Amendment repealed the prohibition of manufacturing, sales and transportation of alcohol in 1933, homebrewing remained illegal on a federal level. That was until H.R. 1337 abolished the federal ban on homebrewing, making every adult free to produce beer for "personal and family use." Thanks to Carter, everyone could relax and have a homebrew.

"No one used this new freedom to greater effect than Charlie Papazian," beer hunter Michael Jackson wrote in 2003. Mere months after Carter signed H.R. 1337, Papazian founded the American Homebrewers Association (AHA), and launched *Zymurgy*, the journal of the AHA, with Charlie Matzen.

Tucked away on page 7 of volume 1, no. 1 of *Zymurgy* was the announcement of the first annual National Homebrew Competition (NHC), with a bit of cheeky vagueness apropos of the homebrewing spirit and Papazian's irreverence: "Sometime during the month of May 1979, in Boulder, Colorado."

True to its word, the first Homebrew Con took place on May 5, 1979, at Boulder's Community Free School, where Papazian had been teaching homebrewing classes. An estimated two hundred people showed up, and thirty-four beer entries were judged. The guys at Boulder Brewing (not yet incorporated) took home a blue ribbon, and Papazian's organizations and advocacy were off and running. In the following years, the NHC would give birth to the Great American Beer Festival (GABF). Aimed at the commercial brewer, the *New Brewer* would join *Zymurgy* as a bimonthly publication. And Papazian's Association of Brewers (AOB) would merge with the Brewers Association of America (BAA) to form the Brewers Association (BA). When it comes to late twentieth-century brewing, all roads lead to Papazian, but more on all that in chapter 9.

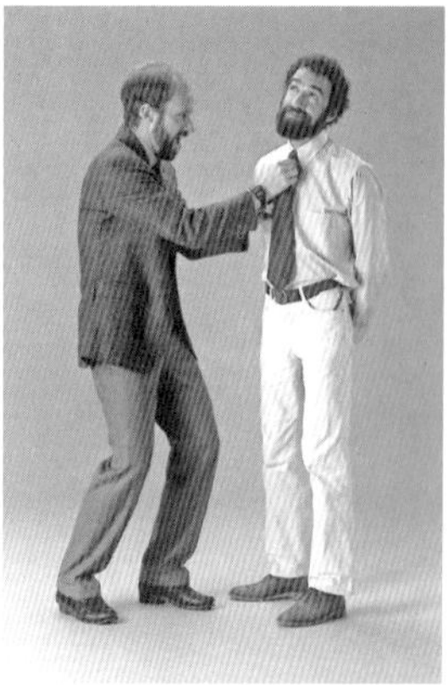

American Homebrewers Association founders Charlie Matzen and Charlie Papazian. *Courtesy Brewers Association.*

"We decided that we would build a one-thousand-square-foot building with an attic, a main floor and a cellar," Ware said. The building would mimic the three-story, gravity-fed system of English breweries, with the grinder in the attic and fermenters in the cellar, "before they had all the modern convenience of electricity."

It would cost roughly $25,000, not to mention more paperwork and a building permit—something Boulder County could easily deny—grinding everything to halt before it even got going. "If we go into Boulder County and say, 'We want to build a brewery,' they're going to say, 'No. Can't do that, nobody's ever done that,'" Ware explained. "If we go in and ask permission to do this, it's going to threaten them, and they're probably not going to have the creativity or inclination to approve it, so let's just build it," Ware told his partners in crime. "We'll have to catch up later with the law."

It helped that they had a federal and state license, which granted them some amount of legitimacy. But after Nelson built the new brewery, there was another hurdle to clear: if they were going to sell beer commercially, they had to get Boulder County Health's approval. And with no building permit, there would be no approval from Boulder County Health.

"They shut us down," Ware said.

So, Ware met with the head of the Boulder County Planning Board. "What do we do?" Ware asked. "We got the building. We got the license. We got this; we got that.

"If they could have just said, 'No,' that would have solved their problem—if we hadn't built the building. But the building was there. What were they going to do with the building? Are they going to force us to tear it down? Or condemn it? What are they going to do? They have to do something....So, it became the type of problem that couldn't just disappear by saying, 'No.'

The planning board's answer to Ware: grease the wheels. Ware hired a recently retired committee member, paid him for six months—"I don't know what he did"—and at the end of the six months, the head of the planning board came back and gave Ware the OK. As the head of the planning board signed the paperwork, he told Ware, "You know, Stick, if you'd come in here and asked me if I would approve building a brewery, I never would have let you do it." If Ware wasn't smiling on the outside, he certainly was on the inside.

On July 4, 1980, the Boulder Brewing Company delivered its first case of Boulder Beer to the Gold Hill Inn—a rustic fine dining restaurant overlooking Boulder Valley. Colorado's craft beer movement had officially begun.

"Something's Going on with the Beer."

The initial lineup leaned on the English tradition: bitter, porter, stout.

"Naturally conditioned, yeast in the bottle, and we were bottling by hand and labeling by hand," Ware said.

"It took hours," Julius recalled. Julius worked summers in the early 1980s when he was home from college. "My lasting contribution was assembling around 1,500 wooden beer cases with Boulder Beer branded into the ends."

Though it was a commercial operation, there was little about it that was "commercial." And within six months, Hummer tasted something he didn't like—something that threatened to shut the whole operation down—lactobacillus. Much like yeast, lactobacillus metabolizes sugar. But unlike yeast, which produces alcohol, lactobacillus produces lactic acid, the kind found in yogurt. In sour beer, this is a welcome, even intended, result. In other beers, it is not. And Boulder Brewing was firmly in the latter category.

"We were starting to distribute and ship, and the bottles were blowing up and gushing and all kinds of problems," Ware said.[4] The answer was sterilization, but they were brewing on a farm using repurposed equipment, which was "really hard to thoroughly sterilize."

Right: Original Boulder Beer crates. *Courtesy Division of Work and Industry, National Museum of American History, Smithsonian Institution.*

Below: Boulder Brewing's original beer labels. *Courtesy Boulder Beer Co.*

Boulder Brewing Company grand opening. *Courtesy Brewers Association.*

Ware said he and Hummer had to take out mortgages to get a loan "to keep things going." But the timing couldn't have been worse between the Iran Hostage Crisis and gunfights at gas stations. "Interest rates, at that time, were 18 percent," Ware said.

"[That] could have been that incident that caused David to remark, 'This is the most irresponsible thing I have ever done,'" Julius said.

They couldn't even pay payroll taxes, and Tom Burns, the brewmaster who replaced Zavatone, left.

"How do I escape this mess I've gotten myself into?" Ware asked. Enter Gerald Smart, a former city planner, real estate salesman and stockbroker who Ware met in a dive shop the previous year.

"He said, 'If you ever need any financial help, give me a call.'" And in the spring of 1983, Ware needed help. He made the call.

"Basically paid off our loan and took control of the company," Ware said. "[He was] going to take us public on the penny stock market."

By the fall of 1983, Smart had guided Boulder Brewing from near financial ruin to rescue. Even if the U.S. Securities and Exchange Commission (SEC) did put the company on ice for three months—Ware gave an interview to a reporter, which the SEC interpreted as "hyping their stock"—delaying Boulder Brewing's public debut into the tumultuous 1984 market. But as Ware pointed out, "There was enough interest in this microbrewery concept that we sold, raised a couple million bucks [$1.7 million] and built the brewery."[5]

Smart was named the president in 1983, and the brewery was relocated from the goat shed to an undeveloped area near Thirtieth Street and Valmont Road. The custom-built 1,200-square-foot brewery was the first building erected in the area.[6] On June 15, 1985, Boulder Brewing—finally residing in its namesake city—celebrated its grand opening with hearty cheers of pale ale and porter.

The move jumped production capacity from six hundred barrels a year to ten thousand (for comparison purposes, Coors was doing 15 million barrels a year), and they installed two fifty-five-gallon copper brewing vessels in the front for all to see.

"I feel there is a piece of history here," Smart told United Press International in 1984. "Whether or not we survive as a beer company, this will be here. This will be the flagship of the microbrewing industry."

Then There Was the Bad Beer

In 1986, the brewery reported that it lost $15,000 on revenues of $403,000.

Back from the British School of Malting and Brewing, Julius started working in the lab on quality control at arguably the brewery's lowest period. "During this time, I was fired twice, only to be rehired a day or two later as the chilly political winds blew through the place," he said, explaining that he was "becoming more and more isolated by the hired management…led by the GM, Skip Miller."

Politics aside, the beer wasn't doing them any favors. Launched in 1986, Ugly Beer, a hazy, unfiltered extra pale ale, was a failed attempt to stand out in a sea of clear, bright lager. "It bombed," wrote Ed Sealover in *Mountain Brew*.[7]

Four years later, Boulder Beer acknowledged the marketing campaign as a failure. And if you can't beat 'em, join 'em. Next up was Sport, a Corona-style knockoff contract brewed in Shiner, Texas.

"It was awful," Julius said. "I was glad to leave."

Mike Lawrence, the fifth president in six years, told the *Boulder Daily Camera* in 1990 that "we prostituted ourselves."

"We went through several rounds of investors/managers," Ware said. "But even with the stock raises, people coming in and investing and then serving a management role, we just couldn't find a really viable management team."

And once again, Boulder Brewing was unable to pay payroll taxes. "The IRS was headed to the door with a padlock," Ware said. The future did not look bright.

2

"THAT BREWPUB STATEMENT."

For years, there were none. Then there was one. And for a decade, Boulder Brewing was the only game in town. But life was not easy for the young brewery. Financial straits proved a constant source of frustration. Additionally, the beer was big in flavor and unusual for most drinkers. Economics has a saying designed to assuage fears of competition: "A rising tide lifts all boats." But for a decade, Boulder Brewing operated without competition and without a tide.

Outside Boulder County, the craft beer revolution was beginning to take hold, inevitably looping Boulder Brewing into a broad cultural movement. With his magazines, festivals, associations and advocacy, Charlie Papazian was always at the center, which made the Front Range all the more invaluable. At least once a year, brewers from all over came to the Great American Beer Festival and made the trek up to Boulder to see the oldest continually operating start-up craft brewery in the nation. They also visited Pearl Street, Boulder's commercial artery, as well as the Hill, a lively stretch of businesses and restaurants one block from the University of Colorado.

They loved the vibrant city and its historically liberal ways. They loved the Flatirons and the climbing opportunities in the surrounding areas. Vast trails were ideal for mountain biking, the music scene was fantastic and the ethos of the city was libertarian. Here, people could follow their bliss any way they saw fit. Here was as good as anywhere to set up shop.

THE WORLD BEER TOUR GOES LOCAL

Though Frank Day was born in Denver, it was Chicago that made his name. The Windy City is where the adman put his Harvard MBA to good use by selling nineteen-cent hot dogs, nine-cent Cokes and nine-cent popcorn. As he told Sealover in *Mountain Brew*, it was an absurdly simple business, and he made "a hell of a lot of money."

Day knew something others didn't. He returned to the Centennial State and opened his first Boulder restaurant, The Walrus, located at 1911 Eleventh Street, in 1973. Day hired Thomas A. Moxcey to run the restaurant, but in 1975, the two went their separate ways. Day held on to The Walrus, and in 1976, he opened the first Old Chicago Pizza and Tap House one block over on Pearl Street.

Serving up deep-dish pizza alongside an array of beer taps seems rudimentary now, but in 1976, collecting 110 different beers, either on draft or in bottles, was a feat—a feat that worked. Boulder was a college town, and a whole lot of people needed places to eat, drink and socialize. Bars work, and so do restaurants. But not everyone attending or visiting the university was born and raised in Colorado. With 110 options to quaff, there was a good chance you were going to find one that reminded you of home.

It also put Day's restaurant in a unique position to capitalize on the burgeoning craft beer movement. The taps were already in place, and the World Beer Tour (considered by many to be the first restaurant loyalty program) introduced adventurous drinkers to different beers and styles from around the globe.

Business boomed. In the 1980s, Day sold The Walrus and immediately repurchased it. He took out the dining tables and replaced them with pool tables, repurposing The Walrus into a college haunt. *Westword*'s Mark Antonation—a student of Fort Collins's Colorado State University—frequented The Walrus during its heyday and described the bar as a top destination for students: "Anyone much over twenty-two looked a little creepy hanging out there."

Day continued to buy more hospitality businesses. Meanwhile, a new brewing model was taking shape in pockets along the West Coast: brewpubs. And why not—the meals were produced on-site, as were the cocktails, so why not the beer? Former geologist and future Denver mayor and Colorado governor John Hickenlooper visited Berkeley's Triple Rock Brewery and Alehouse in 1986. The quality floored him. "I would have driven twenty minutes out of my way without thinking twice about it to have a beer or two

Rock Bottom Restaurant and Brewery

Walnut Brewery became more than a brewpub; it became a prototype. "When they opened up, and it was standing room only," David Zuckerman, brewmaster for Boulder Beer Company from 1990 to 2019, explained, "that's when they realized they had something."

In charge of brewing was Mark Youngquist, a homebrewer from Denver who got his commercial start at the BridgePort Brewing Company in Portland, Oregon, in 1986, before moving back to Colorado and beginning his tenure with Day at Walnut in 1990.

And in November 1991, micro went mainstream when the duo opened their second brewpub, this one in Denver, Rock Bottom Restaurant and Brewery.

Located on Denver's Sixteenth Street Mall, Rock Bottom was housed on the first floor of the Prudential Plaza—an investment company that used the Rock of Gibraltar as its logo. Calling the brewpub Rock Bottom was a play on Prudential's advertising slogan of the time: "Own a piece of the rock."

Rock Bottom was a forerunner of the brewpub explosion that consumed the 1990s and extended well into the 2000s. In *The Audacity of Hops*, author Tom Acitelli described the nine-thousand-square-foot Denver establishment as much a party as it was a restaurant-brewery: "Patrons could see jazz bands and brew kettles simultaneously, and bartenders put on their own show, with twirling glassware and trivia centered around the five beers."

It was a package too good to pass up, and the business expanded rapidly across the nation and went public in 1994. In 1999, Day and a set of new business partners repurchased Rock Bottom and took it private. In the mid- to late 2000s, they opened a headquarters in Louisville, Colorado, and continued to produce a slew of award-winning beers, further spreading the gospel of full-flavored craft brews. Acitelli writes: "They provided perhaps millions of Americans with their first encounters with craft beer. Rock Bottom's four-hundred seat Houston location alone could whet the palates of more consumers in a month than most craft breweries could in a year."

like this," Hickenlooper recounted in his memoir, *The Opposite of Woe*. Two years later, on October 18, 1988, Hickenlooper and his partners, Russell Scherer, Mark Schiffler and Jerry Williams, opened the Wynkoop Brewing Company in Denver's Lower Downtown (LoDo) district. Colorado had its first brewpub.

At Old Chicago, the World Beer Tour was integral to the experience, as it offered drinkers a chance to try beer from everywhere without leaving their neighborhood haunt. The brewpub would be different. It would be as hyper-local as you could get. Similar to the restaurants where diners could see the chefs working away in the kitchen, brewpub drinkers could watch brewers brewing the beer they drank. Not only would the beer have the fullness and the flavor that inspired Hickenlooper to open Wynkoop, but it would also connect beer drinkers with the product in their hands. For the previous six decades, beer was made elsewhere and drunk anywhere. Now the beer would be made and drunk in the same place. The movement was setting down roots.

Once again, Day was first to the party, and Walnut Brewery—located three hundred feet east of The Walrus on Walnut Street—became Boulder's first brewpub. Day and his wife, Gina, called on Moxcey again, and Walnut opened its doors in May 1990.

"Boulder's always been youthful, energetic," George Hanna said. "Even if you're sixty years old in Boulder, you still feel that youthful energy, the influence." It's what drew Hanna to hospitality, pitfalls and all.

Hanna first started working for Day in the mid-1970s, roughly one hundred miles south in Colorado Springs at José Muldoon's, a Tex-Mex restaurant opened in 1974. Originally from Oklahoma, Hanna's grandfather built a cabin in Almont, Colorado—an unincorporated community in the Gunnison National Forest—in the late 1940s. Hanna visited the Centennial State frequently as a boy, eventually relocating in 1970 while touring with his rock 'n' roll band.

But Colorado Springs didn't suit Hanna and his wife, Lynne, and the two moved to Boulder, where they had friends and Day had a project. "And Walnut was the project," Hanna said.

For a year and a half, Hanna was the general manager of Walnut Brewery, more than enough time to see how well Boulder responded to full-flavored beer. Hanna was a restaurateur at heart—"I don't brew, and I've never cheffed"—and quickly realized that if Boulder Brewing could make it, if Walnut could make it, surely there was room for a third.

Lunchtime at the Oasis

Hanna's Oasis Brewer Pub set up shop two blocks south of Walnut Brewery, at 1095 Canyon Boulevard, and featured distinct Egyptian décor and likewise-themed beers: Capstone Extra Special Bitter, Scarab Red Ale, Tut Brown Ale, Zoser Stout and so on, similar to the lineups Walnut and Boulder Brewing were putting out but still relatively unknown to average beer drinkers.

"Early folks in the business really had to fight that stigma," Hanna said. "Full-bodied, full-flavor, big beers, more alcohol....It's really what was going on in England."

English-influenced and inspired ales were commonplace in the burgeoning craft beer marker for a variety of reasons. Ales ferment at a higher temperature than lagers and for considerably less time—a few days as opposed to a few weeks—which makes them cheaper to produce. The ability to turn tank space is crucial for those starting out. If you're going to serve beer, you better have a lot on hand. Additionally, ales are easier to brew—or, more accurately, easier to conceal off flavors or inconsistencies. And probably most important, ales are wildly different in color, aroma and flavor than the German-influenced macro lagers on the market. If you were going to persuade a drinker in the early 1990s to try something new, something different and, more often than not, something more expensive, you'd have better luck with a beer significantly different rather than a beer slightly similar.

It worked like gangbusters.

"Something Was Missing."

"Every other brewpub in the country had five beers," Kevin Daly, cofounder of Mountain Sun Pub & Brewery, said. "There was an amber, a golden, a stout, a porter and a seasonal.

"[Our idea] was to feature our five or six beers and then have a bunch of guest beers from California," he continued. These were beers like Red Tail Ale from Mendocino Brewing Company and Sierra Nevada Brewing Company's Pale Ale.

"Which was really unusual," Daly pointed out—not even bars carried more than three micros at once.

The idea paid off because when Mountain Sun Pub & Brewery opened on October 5, 1993, the John Cross brewing system Daly acquired was cold. Guest beers were all you could drink on opening day. "Our brewery was broken at first," Daly said. "Something was missing."

Daly wasn't the only brewer in town with a John Cross system. Four miles east, on Arapaho Avenue, Adam Avery was also getting his brewery up and running using a similar system designed from repurposed Grundy tanks.

Grundys, mass-produced tanks from the 1950s and 1960s, were popular storage vessels in United Kingdom pubs until pub owners found ways to pry off the lids and water down the beer. Brewers switched to secure kegs, and the California-based Cross bought the discarded Grundy tanks cheap and flooded burgeoning American breweries with them.

Luckily for Daly, it didn't take brewer Jack Harris long to get the Cross system up and running. In November, he debuted Mountain Sun's first house beer: Colorado Kind Ale (an ESB/hoppy-amber hybrid).

Mountain Sun's presence on Pearl Street—about a block and a half from the pedestrian foot mall—signaled a change in the Boulder brewing scene. Boulder Brewing paved the way for Frank Day, Old Chicago led to the Walnut and the Walnut inspired Hanna's Oasis. But Daly's Mountain Sun was different. Originally hailing from the East Coast, Daly first set foot in Boulder in 1990 while visiting his sister on his way to Portland, Oregon. At the time, Lewis and Clark Law School was Daly's destination, but Boulder soon beckoned him back.

Kevin Daly and Ian Blackford. *Courtesy Mountain Sun Pubs & Breweries.*

"I was really unhappy at law school and did not want to be an attorney," Daly said. "And was trying to figure out what I was doing while I was sitting in these McMenamins Pubs." Established by Mike and Brian McMenamin in 1985, McMenamins was Oregon's first brewpub. The model caught on and expanded to several locations, including theaters and hotels.

Located just a few steps from the Willamette River, McMenamins Fulton

Pub & Brewery was replete with warm wood and colorful décor. Daly knew the Portland staple would work beautifully in the People's Republic of Boulder. He already had a partner in crime, Ian Blackford, and a love for hospitality—the two were Deadheads and used to sell beer in the parking lots of Grateful Dead shows.

"We used to sell stuff so we could go to more shows," Daly said. It's not exactly legal but undoubtedly effective if the only goal is to see more Grateful Dead concerts. But they would need something more stable if they wanted to make a living. It came down to two options: a bagel bakery or a brewery. The former would cost $250,000—more than either could borrow from their parents. But when Blackford learned that the McMenamins opened their first pub for $150,000, the latter seemed doable.

It took a year for the two to locate a spot, 1535 Pearl Street, coincidentally, a former music store. Harris, whom they snagged from McMenamins, got their broken brewing system up and running, and Mountain Sun found its legs.

"We didn't have to worry about cash flow," Daly said. "It was just trying to learn at twenty-four how to run a business."

"Really? A Brewery?"

James, Chris and Mark Heinritz and Cameron Stainton were all between twenty-four and twenty-eight when they handed over every penny they had and promised a whole lot more to Herbie Kauvar, owner of the Sink on the Hill.

The date was September 20, 1992, and owning a historic dive bar one block from CU seemed like a great idea. It was, and four years later, Chris and Mark Heinritz branched out to the Pearl Street Mall and opened RedFish Fish House & Brewery at 2027 Thirteenth Street, in the summer of 1996. Six years before, Boulder had zero brewpubs. Now it had four within a mile radius.

The fifth would come from without.

Bob Hesser was a beer geek and a homebrewer, and he had a simple piece of advice for Alex Puchner: There's a vacant building on Pearl Street, and it's ideal for a brewpub.

"Really?" Puchner asked. "I'll go check it out." Puchner had a background in brewpubs, and he was looking to open a new one. The Southern California–based restaurant chain BJ's Chicago Pizzeria had come calling. It wanted into the brewing business, and Puchner was the man to do it.

BJ's brewhouse behind the bar. *Courtesy of BJ's Restaurant & Brewhouse.*

Founded in 1978 in Santa Ana by Mike Phillips and Bill Cunningham, BJ's Chicago Pizzeria was to the Golden State what Day's Old Chicago was to the Centennial.

But by 1995, Day and Moxcey were outpacing the competition. In the previous twelve months, the duo had opened twelve restaurants, bringing their total to five Rock Bottom Breweries and twelve Old Chicago restaurants. In almost two decades, BJ's had expanded to eight stores. If BJ's was going to compete, it had to brew its own beer, and it would need to do it in Day's backyard.

The stage was set, and Puchner was in the spotlight. The 1995 Great American Beer Festival brought him to Denver, and Hesser's tip took him to Boulder.

"I'm on Pearl Street, and I see this vacant building," Puchner said. "I'm kind of peeking in the window, looking around, and the landlord is inside." The landlord, Dave Welker, was a member of the American Homebrewers Association.

"Welker comes outside and says, 'Hey, you interested?'" Puchner said. "'Well, actually, yeah. I'm with the BJ's Restaurant chain, and we're interested in building a brewery. This looks like a good location here in Boulder.'

"And he said, 'Really? A brewery?'" Welker loved the idea of a brewpub. Phillips and Cunningham loved the idea of a BJ's on the Pearl Street Mall. In the fall of 1995, the lease was signed, but Boulder would have to wait. In 1996, the pizza chain went public, bought Pietro's Pizza in Oregon and broke ground on its Brea, California facility. Brea became BJ's first microbrewery. Boulder had to settle for second, but not Bob Hesser. The man with the tip became BJ's on Pearl's first brewmaster when the restaurant and brewery opened in February 1997.

"It Got Crazy."

Boulder's brewpub scene was jamming: Walnut, Oasis, Mountain Sun, RedFish and BJ's—all within a one-mile radius.

"Those were neat times," Puchner said.

"It got crazy," Hanna said. "Boulder responded very well to Oasis. And drinking."

"A lot of serious beer drinkers there," Puchner said. "It's one of the best craft beer markets in the country, if not the world."

And the scene was exploding.

"One year, I think it was '95, just as we were trying to open the new facility, the brewpub hit five thousand barrels—the second-largest production in the nation at that time for a brewpub," Hanna said. "And it was all done on a seven-barrel system."

Hanna needed a second brewery, one dedicated to production and packaging. The Oasis Brewery Annex, located two miles east on Walnut Street, would be it—twelve thousand square feet, enough to produce beer for Boulder and beyond.

"Around '94, '95, we were really selling a lot of beer," he continued. "We started packaging, hand-bottling and everything at that point, but we were seeing a demand for our kegs, and we started distributing with a local distributor, state distributor. And it started going really quickly." According to Hanna's estimates, Oasis brewed about ten thousand barrels a year at its peak—an enormous sum for the time.

"If you really had something, you caught a little traction. You get some investors and people willing to put some money into equipment, especially back then because there wasn't much," Hanna said.

Brewing is a capital-intensive proposition: before you can sell beer, you have to produce it. And production doesn't just involve raw materials but also physical space. Be it kegs (a half-barrel of beer) or large tanks for brewing, fermenting, conditioning and storage, real estate is required. And real estate is always limited and always expensive. For Hanna, the Annex was the answer. For Puchner, the brewpub on Pearl is all he had to work with.

"I'll be the first to admit, it was a terrible design," Puchner says of BJ's layout, which incorporated tanks behind the bar and two floors of production.

"Having the mill up those stairs, and having no silo or auger and having to haul those fifty-pound sacks [of grain] up two flights was just ridiculous," he said. "But the other ridiculous thing was the brewhouse right behind the bar."

The restaurant business was changing. Whether you went to Spago on the Sunset Strip or to a Subway sandwich shop anywhere in America, you could watch your food being cooked and assembled. Brewpubs followed suit when it came to beer. "It's how we designed them," Puchner said. "The idea is that the brewer would be very social and talk to the guests at the bar."

At first, when business was steady, it might have helped break down customers' hesitations to try something different, something new. But the brewing business in Boulder was anything but steady. It was busy as hell.

"You got bartenders tripping over your hoses," Puchner said. "And it's dangerous because you're dealing with chemicals—that was the last time I ever designed a brewery like that." Nowadays, most brewpub breweries are behind glass or isolated in some capacity for safety reasons. But back then, "it was pretty common," Puchner said.

Imitation and inspiration were also common. When Puchner scouted Pearl Street in 1995, he stopped in Mountain Sun, Oasis and Walnut for inspiration. He found that inspiration, particularly Walnut's beer logos, on the wall.

"We basically stole that from them," Puchner said. "We loved that look. So, when we started brewing beer, first in our Brea location, then Boulder, then Portland and elsewhere, we modeled a lot of the interior of our restaurants after that look," he said. "That brewpub statement."

3

EAST OF PEARL, WEST OF THE RESERVOIR

Meanwhile, Back at Boulder Brewing...

"The IRS was headed to the door with a padlock," Randolph Ware said. Colorado's first craft brewery was in trouble again, and unpaid payroll taxes threatened to sink the place once more. Ware had left the board, as had Hummer. Six ownership groups in five years had been through the brewery, and as Sealover wrote in *Mountain Brew*, "full-time staff had shrunk from twenty-six to six in just two years."

"But for several years, Frank Day had been kind of circling," Ware said, "keeping track of what was going on."

And Day was there when the Internal Revenue Service came knocking. Day asked how much they owed.

"[Day] wrote a check and got control of the brewery," Ware said.

Colorado's first craft brewery lived to see another day.

"It's not as easy to be around for forty years as some people might think," Jeff Brown said in 2019.

Originally from Winter Haven, Florida, Brown relocated to Illinois as a teenager and then started working in the restaurant business with Day in 1969. In 1974, Brown changed states again, first to Colorado Springs and then to Boulder in 1980, where he partnered with Day to open Boulder's José Muldoon's, an expansion of the successful Tex-Mex restaurant Day started in Colorado Springs.

Working for Day in one capacity meant you worked for Day in any capacity. There was no telling where you'd end up next. And for Brown, Boulder Brewing was next.

Frank and Gina Day, along with partners Bob and Diane Greenlee,[8] bought Boulder Brewing, took the company private, changed the name to Boulder Beer Company, added a kitchen and tapped Brown as the general manager. Gina and Diane took over day-to-day operations.

They also hired David Zuckerman of Portland's BridgePort Brewing Company to be the brewery's next brewmaster. "I was a life-long Oregonian, until twenty-nine years ago," Zuckerman said in 2019.

Born in Stockton, California, Zuckerman studied international affairs at Lewis and Clark College in Portland between stints abroad. Across the pond, Zuckerman picked up a taste for English pub culture and full-flavor ales, which, in the 1980s, were finding a toehold in Portland's pub community. There was the Horse Brass Pub, established in 1976 and run by Don Younger, and McMenamins Hillsdale Pub, the brothers' first brewpub (opened in February 1984).

"The entire establishment was called Hillsdale Pub, but the brewing part of it was called Captain Neon's Fermentation Chamber," Zuckerman told Theresa McCulla of the Smithsonian Institution in 2017. "It was all psychedelic artwork and kind of old beat-up dairy equipment, but that's where I had the epiphany that somebody could show up into that room and make beer and that people such as myself would show up and drink it.

"It's the first time it disconnected beer from being a commodity-, factory-driven product produced by anonymous people that you have no hope of ever meeting, in a process you'd have no hope of ever seeing," Zuckerman continued. "And here it is, right in front of the drinker." For Zuckerman, the experience "glommed the two," production and consumption. People made beer, and Zuckerman wanted to be one of them.

Luckily, Zuckerman had a friend in the business, Mark Youngquist. And Youngquist was working at BridgePort.

"My first real job in the beer industry was working in pubs in London," Zuckerman said. "I already had the interest in beer, but that's where I was first able to handle beer—in a professional manner, but it was retail." His job at BridgePort wasn't much more. "Making pizzas and serving beers," Zuckerman told McCulla. "I loved the flavors they were making, and I loved talking about beer, and the clientele who came in were interested in beer."

But love from a distance can only last so long. Separating the pub and the brewing operations was a pane of glass. Zuckerman could look through and see "where my ambition was." And after three or four months of pulling pints and slinging pies, Zuckerman quit.

"I told the pub manager I was quitting to get a job brewing," Zuckerman told McCulla. "And I went to the next desk over and told Karl Ockert that I just quit, and I need a job. And so, I started working part-time there."

There's no such thing as parttime in a brewery, and Zuckerman's role expanded to a full-time brewer's assistant. Then Youngquist called; he'd left BridgePort and relocated in Boulder to headup brewing at Walnut. When Youngquist heard Day and company had bought Boulder Brewing, he knew they would need a brewer, and Zuckerman seemed like the guy. Zuckerman agreed, made the trek, interviewed and was offered the job. It took all of two weeks, and on August 1, 1990, David Zuckerman joined the Boulder Beer Company.

Brewing in the '90s

"The '90s were really about small brewers inserting themselves into something that had been, predominantly, players of large commercial operations," Brown said. "The industry and the legislative side of the industry were still trying to figure out: was this kind of small, boutique industry something that would get its legs under it and eventually spread its wings? Or was it just going to be—as some people thought at the time—just a fad that was just going to go into the history books?"

The answer was a little bit of both. Craft brewing was destined for the history books, both as a fad—future shakeups and shakeouts would thin the brewing herd multiple times—and as a longstanding industry. And though brewpubs proliferated the Front Range (and in other legislative-friendly states outside Colorado), they were more restaurants than breweries. As Mountain Sun's Kevin Daly explained, "The brewery is one-third of what we do....Actually, one-fourth. It's the service, the food, the atmosphere and the beer."

But the roots were beginning to stretch beyond brewpubs and beyond Downtown Boulder. For Boulder County's brewing scene to branch out, small start-ups needed to start pushing the envelope.

Enter Gordon Knight.

Born on February 20, 1950, in Scottsbluff, Nebraska, Knight was an army man, a helicopter pilot in Vietnam and a Purple Heart recipient.

Incorporated at the tail end of 1992, Knight's High Country Brewing—located in a small industrial space three miles east of Boulder Beer—was the first non-brewpub brewery to open in the county since Boulder Brewing started at the goat shed. But unlike Boulder Brewing, Knight didn't have to cobble his brewery together: he could buy one used. The industry had evolved to the point that brewing equipment was for sale secondhand, and Knight became the second owner of Colorado's most important brewing system.[9]

"Gordon was a small-framed guy, a bit nervous in his motions, very observant, somewhat introspective, and very engaging with his eyes and facial expressions," Jeff Lebesch of New Belgium Brewing told *Brewbound* in 2011. "We toured around the brewery and garage while I explained the use of all the brewhouse, malt handling, fermentation, chilling, filling and storage equipment....By the conclusion of the tour, Gordon was fairly overloaded with information and was wandering around the yard with his hands in his pockets and staring at the ground. Finally, with little hesitation, he yanked his hands out of his pockets, turned his palms to the sky, looked straight at me and said 'Why not, let's do it.'"

Knight moved Lebesch's system to 6270 Arapahoe Road in Boulder and started brewing. It wouldn't stay there long. Knight partnered with Ed Grueff; moved the brewery thirty-six miles northwest to Estes Park, a picturesque mountain town located in Rocky Mountain National Park; renamed it Estes Park Brewery; and sold it to Grueff.

"[Knight] was never really good at establishing breweries," Bob Baile, president of Twisted Pine Brewing Company, said. "He liked to start breweries."

And Knight had plenty of opportunities to enjoy the start-up. Opened in 1993, High Country/Estes Park Brewery sold to Grueff in 1994, and Twisted Pine sold to Baile in 1996. In June 1997, Knight and Jim Parker opened Wolf Tongue Brewery in Nederland, Colorado—about seventeen miles due west from Boulder. In 1999, Parker left Colorado for the Oregon brewing scene, and Knight closed Wolf Tongue in 2001.

Brewing beer is a labor-intensive job, and Knight was doing it alone. That's hard, but for a lot of people, managing a company and workers is even harder. That was the situation Gina Day, Brown and Zuckerman found themselves in at Boulder Beer. For Zuckerman, it was "bipolar."

"There was new ownership with the old staff," Zuckerman said. "And some of the old staff [brewmaster, sales manager, brewer, mechanic, packaging crew] was the ownership of the old company.

Gordon Knight (1950–2002)

"Though small in stature and tiny in his brewery operation, Gordon was big in the Colorado scene and loved by all," Lebesch told *Brewbound* in 2011. "His beers were great, and he was one of the first in the country to produce a pleasing super-hop beer. Most memorable for me is his way of setting out to do his own thing in the brewing business; he was a leader in his own unique way and never a follower."

Gordon Knight. *Courtesy Oskar Blues Brewery.*

Knight was also the first to win three GABF gold medals for three different beers from three different breweries: Estes Park Brewery's Renegade Red in the India Pale Ale category in 1993, Twisted Pine Brewing Company's Twisted Amber in the American Amber Ale category in 1996 and Wolf Tongue Brewery's Coffee Porter in the Brown Porter category in 1998.

"Gordon was a meticulous brewer," Baile said. "Beer did not touch the brewery floor. If you were going to take a hose off a fitting, he had a little piece of Tupperware underneath it so the beer would spill into the Tupperware. He was meticulous. You could perform surgery in his brewery."

A brewer by trade and a pilot by identity, Knight continued to fly. And Knight was flying on July 30, 2002, fighting the Big Elk fire northwest of Lyons, when he died in a helicopter crash. He was fifty-two.

"One of the final decisions, or choices from the [previous management] company, was to send a truckload of beer to California to hit month-end numbers," Zuckerman said. Only problem was that the beer didn't have a customer waiting in California. "I knew what they were doing, and I just kind of shook my head and thought, alright, well, you will be judged on how this turns out. And, sure enough, five days later, we got a call from the distributor in Sacramento saying, 'Hey, a truckload of beer showed up that we didn't order. What's going on?'"

Enough was enough. Mass firing of the old guard cleaned house, and Zuckerman cleaned up the beers. He switched from Whitbread—a dried yeast strain from Scotland—to Wyeast, a liquid yeast strain produced in Oregon (Wy'east is the Multnomah name for Oregon's Mount Hood), tweaked the recipes for Boulder Porter, Extra Pale and Amber and introduced Singletrack Rye Pale Ale and Buffalo Gold Golden Ale.

Despite the success and accessibility of Buffalo Gold, Boulder Beer still had hurdles in its way. "Our setup was unusual," Zuckerman said. Boulder Beer was essentially a manufacturing facility with a brewpub license. "We could pour beer. We could sample beer. We could sell beer to go. We were able to distribute beer."

But Zuckerman added, "It didn't do us a whole lot of good originally. Because there was nobody out here [East Boulder], and nobody knew what we were and what we were doing."

"YOUR HOMEBREW'S PRETTY GOOD."

"In 1990, there was a lot of influx of people from outside of Colorado, and they were bringing their tastes with them," Zuckerman said.

"Whether it's rock climbing or beer drinking," Baile said, "Boulder is for the adventurous." Adam Avery was both. He loved rock climbing and drinking beer. And he hated the idea of being a lawyer. At twenty-seven years old, the prospective law student was staring down the barrel of a mid-twenties crisis.

"Your homebrew's pretty good; you might want to think about that," Avery's climbing buddies told him. He had to admit, it sounded a hell of a lot better than being a lawyer.

Born in Macomb, Illinois, and raised in Decatur, Avery came to Colorado in 1984 for Regis College. Soon, the mountains called, and Avery started climbing. Hobby led to profession, and Avery started working at the sports-apparel company Eastern Mountain Sports before taking the law school admission test. He did well and was accepted to the University of Denver's Sturm Law School, but something didn't seem right. His friends had started practicing and waved him off.

"They were like, 'Man, there is no way you're going to enjoy this,'" Avery said.

Introductory Styles

Before the craft beer revolution, America's beverage was monochromatic at best. "It was: what degree of yellow are you hoping for?" Zuckerman said. Then came a spectrum of brews. Some were dark and murky, and others came with hues ranging from vibrant pale to rich mahogany. And when bartenders plopped down these pints amid seas of fizzy yellow light lager, craft popped.

But curiosity will only get you so far. If brewers wanted to convince dedicated drinkers to switch brands, they needed to provide a flavor profile that was different yet familiar, encouraging yet accessible. They needed a helping hand, and Boulder Beer had an answer: Buffalo Gold Golden Ale.

Developed by Youngquist at Walnut Brewery, Buffalo Gold sported a deep gold color, a soft malt profile reminiscent of honey nut cereal and a hint of floral hops. Buffalo Gold had enough but not too much. For diehard light beer drinkers—who shopped more by brand than taste—Buffalo Gold was a beer they could get behind. For new entrants to the beer world, Buffalo Gold held open the door.

A year or two later, another beer would do the same—this time as an amber: New Belgium's Fat Tire.

"Colorado was amber beer driven," Eric Wallace, cofounder of Longmont's Left Hand Brewing Company, said. "If you didn't have an amber, you were nobody." Again, color helped amber stand out from the pack, but with a malt profile of toasty biscuit mingling with sweet butterscotch, and hoppy notes of fresh pine, amber ales encouraged beer drinkers who didn't think of themselves as beer drinkers.

A glass of Nitro Sawtooth Ale at Left Hand Brewing Company. *Author photo.*

There were others: Tabernash Brewery in Denver led with a hefeweizen, a German-style wheat ale. It didn't catch fire like Portland's Widmer Brothers Brewing Hefe, but the soft, hazy ale enticed many. Similarly, Coors opened a brewery, the Sandlot, inside the newly constructed Coors Field in 1995 and started brewing a Belgian wit called Belly Slide. It became a smashing success and was renamed Blue Moon when Coors took the sparkling ale with wafts of fresh oranges and cracked coriander to market. And thanks to Coors's large production facility and extensive distribution channels, Blue Moon traveled far and converted many.

So, Avery fell back on another Colorado hobby he had picked up: homebrewing.

The date: January 28, 1990. The place: a friend's Super Bowl party. The San Francisco 49ers beat the Denver Broncos fifty-five to ten in the Louisiana Superdome to collect their fourth Vince Lombardi Trophy while the Broncos netted their fourth loss on the championship stage. But Denver's loss was Colorado's gain; Avery discovered homebrew, a full-bodied brown ale that kicked open something in his mind.

"The next day, I went out and bought a homebrew kit," Avery told McCulla in 2017. Avery was infatuated and became the type of homebrewer who had "three batches going at once." He was brewing so much that he gave it away at climbing sites to anyone who would take it.

"At the same time, the spring of '93, my dad [Larry Avery] took early retirement," Avery said.

Avery wasn't the only one in his family to relocate to the Centennial State; his sister Angie attended CU's law school, and Larry often visited. Larry was a runner and a devoted one at that. But in the early 1990s, Boulder wasn't the running mecca Larry hoped for. Boulder should have a proper running store, Larry resolved, and moved west to follow his bliss.

But finding a storefront for a running shop was easier said than done. "[Larry] couldn't get it set up," Avery said.

Like father, like son, Avery was also looking for a place to stake his claim. Avery knew he couldn't work for Eastern Mountain Sports forever, and law school was a no-go. What was a twenty-seven-year-old to do? Start a brewery, of course.

"I had a business plan together," Avery said. "Been shopping it around to people and had some people who wanted to put money in it."

Adam Avery, circa 1994. *Courtesy Avery Brewing Co.*

Larry Avery, circa 1994. *Courtesy Avery Brewing Co.*

Brewing? Larry wasn't so sure. "I didn't think it was a good idea because all I had ever drank was Budweiser, Miller and Coors, and I didn't want to compete with them," Larry said in 2017. "However, when I'd come out to visit, Adam would take me to Walnut Brewery and Wynkoop Brewery....I drank those beers, and I drank Adam's homebrew, which was good."

Avery had passion and interested investors. Larry had a business partner and some capital. The beer business beckoned. "He and his partner who were going to do the running store came to me and said, 'Hey, we'll bankroll it, we'll split thirds.'" Avery said. "And we got started on $90,000."

On September 1, 1993, the Avery Brewing Co. incorporated in a two-thousand-square-foot warehouse at 5763 Arapahoe Avenue—three miles southeast of Boulder Beer and one mile west of High Country.

"I really, you know, walked in kind of blindly," Avery told McCulla. "I'd never worked in a brewery before."

Avery started on a seven-barrel John Cross system, the same one Daly and company were using at Mountain Sun, and Avery stopped by to see how things were working for them. He also swung by High Country to talk to Knight. And with a little help from Jim Hall, a climbing buddy working at Boulder Beer, Avery got his commercial brewing legs under him. From September to December 1993, Avery brewed test batches while Larry helped cut the concrete and pour the slab and drains. When Avery Brewing Co. opened for business in 1994, it had three beers: Redpoint Ale (an amber), Ellie's Brown Ale and Out of Bound Stout. The stout won gold at the 1994 GABF later that year.

"The Incestuousness of Boulder County Breweries and Its Effect on Its Progeny."

Ask Twisted Pine's president Bob Baile to show you around the brewery, and he'll excitedly point out tanks he's acquired from Avery and Left Hand, a mash tun from New Belgium, a glycol tank from a brewery he can't remember and a brewing-in-the-'90s staple: a John Cross seven-barrel brewhouse.

"I once gave a talk entitled 'The Incestuousness of Boulder County Breweries and Its Effect on Its Progeny,'" Baile said, "and how all of us shared equipment and recipes and the desire to make good beer—but especially the equipment."

Jeff Lebesch's touring brewery, housed in Fort Collins at New Belgium Brewery. *Courtesy New Belgium Brewing.*

Raised in Jersey City, New Jersey, and armed with a degree in biochemistry, Baile made his way to the Centennial State in 1978 as a research chemist for an area pharmaceutical company. "I tell everyone I went from making drugs to making beer," Baile said, recounting how a chance meeting with What's Brewin' Homebrew Supply and Liquor Mart's manager, Paul Gatza, opened Baile's mind to beer.[10]

"[Gatza] couldn't have been nicer," Baile continued. "He spent a lot of time talking to me about how to homebrew. At that time, it was almost entirely syrups. They had a few grains, but Paul was extremely gracious and got me hooked."

Baile loved homebrewing and decided to go commercial. Like brewers before him, Baile toured the area for information and inspiration. But when Baile stopped into Estes Park Brewery, he found more than he bargained for.

"Their equipment was for sale," Baile said. "So, I wound up buying their equipment, and I started a brewery in my garage in Rollinsville." The equipment was Lebesch's original New Belgium system that Knight bought and sold to Grueff. The year was 1995, and the system was now on its fourth brewery—Baile's Peak to Peak Brewing Company.

"So, I got to know [Knight] because I bought that equipment," Baile said. "I called him one day, and I said, 'Hey, do you mind if I stop in and just chat about some of the nuances?'" Knight was amenable, and the two grew close. Then, in late 1996, Knight told Baile he was going to sell Twisted Pine.

"You don't have to go very far," Baile responded. "I wound up buying it and merged the two." Baile ditched the Peak to Peak name and kept Twisted Pine. He also relocated the Lebesch system—now on its fifth brewery in as many years—to Twisted Pine's 2,500-square-foot location on Valmont Road.

BREWING IN BOULDER'S BACKYARD

The craft beer industry was going bananas—from fewer than three hundred U.S. breweries at the beginning of the 1990s to over fifteen hundred by the end. Back in Boulder, only two breweries were operating in 1990. Nine years later, that number had climbed to ten.

Not all were successes. Two, Beartooth Brewing Company and Far Superior Brewing Co., came and went while the revolution started setting roots across the county. Guys like Dale Katechis would enter the scene in

SELF-DISTRIBUTION AND THE THREE-TIERED SYSTEM

In addition to the repeal of Prohibition, the Twenty-First Amendment ushered in the era of the three-tiered system for the manufacture and sale of alcoholic beverages. In essence, brewers manufacture the product (first tier) and sell it to wholesalers (second tier), who then distribute it to the retail outlets, such as liquor stores, restaurants and bars (third tier).

The system was designed to both prohibit monopolies of all three tiers—effectively creating tide-houses—while governing the excessive consumption that led to Prohibition in the first place.*

However, Section Two of the Twenty-First Amendment stipulated that "the transportation or importation into any State, Territory, or possession of the United States for delivery or use therein of intoxicating liquors, in violation of the laws thereof, is hereby prohibited." In essence, the power to control alcohol resided with the state. And each state had widely different liquor laws. The one that benefitted Colorado brewers the most was the ability to sell directly to their customers—pints over the bar or packaged beer to go—in addition to selling packaged beer to wholesalers.

"Vital access to market is the number-one reason Colorado has become the state of craft beer," John Carlson, executive director of the Colorado Brewers Guild, said in a 2016 interview with *ColoradoBiz*.

* The author recognizes that there was a host of factors that contributed to Prohibition beyond excessive consumption but lacks the space to delve into them here. For more information on that era, please consult Daniel Okrent's book-length study of the period, *Last Call: The Rise and Fall of Prohibition*. For readers interested in Colorado's role in the "great experiment," consult Jason Hanson's "The First Draft: Colorado History Over a Few Beers" in the May 2, 2019 issue of *Colorado Heritage Magazine*.

Boulder and head north to start Oskar Blues Brewery in the quiet town of Lyons in 1997. That same year, Knight would head to Nederland to open his third brewery, Wolf Tongue. Kevin Daly was thinking of expanding Mountain Sun, and Oasis's George Hanna was thinking of getting out.

Meanwhile, Colorado's first craft brewery saw tremendous growth. "Between 1990 and 1994, company sales grew by more than 800 percent," Sealover wrote of Boulder Beer in *Mountain Brew*. "Production jumped from three thousand barrels a year to more than twenty thousand."

The changes Gina Day, Brown and Zuckerman put in place worked. The beer was better, the management was consistent and Brown found opportunities in a market interested in choice.

"We were at the forefront of convincing restaurateurs and liquor retailers," Brown said. He would also tell bar owners, "If you'd open up more space, you'd just be giving your consumers better choices, more choices."

Much of that was thanks to Colorado's access to the market.

"It was really a handful of us, back in the mid-'90s, that more or less lobbied the state legislature to allow us to continue to do business," Brown said. "A lot of that was access to market with self-distribution."

Distributors disagreed. They saw smaller breweries self-distributing as a breach of the three-tiered system. "We didn't look at it that way," Brown said. "We simply approached it as we're not really circumventing the three-tiered, just maintaining small brewer access." And that access made Colorado fertile soil for future breweries. Boulder Beer was growing, and it was time to rebrand and broaden appeal. In 1993, Boulder Beer Company became Rockies Brewing Company—the same year the state welcomed a major-league baseball team of the same name.

Brewing in Boulder was going mainstream.

4
DOUBLE AUGHT EXPANSION

Big Beers and Bigger Businesses

"It took about nine years to actually turn a profit," Adam Avery said. "It wasn't like we were hemorrhaging cash, but there were three years where Dad and I didn't pay ourselves."

Opened in early 1994 to a booming market, Avery Brewing Co. had to crawl before it could run. Its initial lineup—RedPoint Amber Ale, Out of Bounds Stout and Ellie's Brown Ale—wasn't catching on.[11] Writing in 2010, beer scribe Stan Hieronymus described Ellie's as "typical of the early beers from Avery in the mid-1990s—technically excellent and somewhat bold by Colorado standards, but nothing that created a buzz with aficionados."

"The beers at the time that were killing it were Fat Tire, 90 Shilling, Sawtooth," Avery said. "Beers like that…good-drinking beers."

Avery's amber was a big amber, "more like an IPA," by his estimation. Ten years later, a brewery wouldn't survive without an IPA on the tap list. But when Avery started making his in 1996, bartenders would call him up and complain: Come pick up your beer. It's too bitter.

It almost sunk him. "It came to a point, do-or-die kind of thing," Avery recounted. "We're going to make a big monster beer that's highly hopped, highly bitter, highly alcoholic." When Larry Avery came across a bike race named "Hog Heaven" in the local newspaper, they had their name.

Released in 1998, Hog Heaven was brewed with Columbus hops, two-row barley and caramel malts. Big, rich and piney, Hog Heaven didn't fit any particular style at the time—it weighed in at 9.2 percent alcohol by volume and sported over one hundred international bittering units—so Avery put "Dry-hopped Barleywine-style ale" on the label.

"Now most people want to call it a double IPA," Avery told Hieronymus. "Back then I'd never heard of the term 'double IPA.'"[12]

"We talk about Hog's the beer that saved the brewery," Avery said. "And it really was because it got us in with out-of-state distribution."

Hog Heaven was the beer that finally created a much-needed buzz with aficionados, particularly with Tomme Arthur of California's Pizza Port Brewing.[13] Pizza Port was hosting a strong ale festival, and Arthur wanted to pour Hog Heaven. Avery agreed. At the fest, another brewer drank Hog, Greg Koch of Stone Brewing in Escondido. Koch was self-distributing Stone beer and wanted to bring on other brands. He asked Avery if he would like to be the first. Again, Avery agreed. This pig had flown.

"If not *the* beer that turned it around, it was the mentality of how we should use our brewery to do what we want to do," Avery said. And what Avery wanted to do was push the envelope.

"Truly doing that," Avery said, "making beers for a very, very small and select group of people, who, I believe, were looking for that sort of thing."

One big beer led to another. Next came The Reverend, a Belgian-style quadrupel ale, and then Salvation, a Belgian-style golden ale.[14] Along with Hog, these formed Avery's holy trinity of ales. "I wanted to do those big beers, and I wanted to experiment," Avery said. "That was *my* piece of the craft industry—to drive that segment."

Drinkers agreed. Avery's line of big beers caught fire and exploded production—from three thousand barrels in 1999 to fifteen thousand barrels in 2009. Throughout those years, Avery found himself on the "tip of the spear," and he continued to push the brewery to try new things. From an IPA in 1996, when it was deemed so bitter that customers refused to drink it, to his lauded imperial IPA, The Maharaja, in 2002.

"I ran the company for a long time as a hobby gone berserk," Avery said. "And, literally, doing everything I wanted. And then finding people who were like-minded."

Andy Parker was one of those like-minded people. A homebrewer since he was nineteen, Parker brewed his way across the country—even to Hawaii—and back. Parker joined Avery in 2002, and in 2003, Avery started a barrel program. Over the following years, the program would expand by leaps and bounds, but back in 2003, an American brewery with a barrel program was an outlier. Then, in 2004, came The Beast—the first installment of

AMERICAN-STYLE INDIA PALE ALE

First developed in England in the mid-1800s, hop-forward India pale ale (IPA) took a while to catch on with American drinkers. Out in Chico, California, Sierra Nevada Brewing Company popularized Cascade hops with its pale ale as early as 1980. It sported thirty-eight international bittering units (IBUs). In San Francisco, Anchor Brewing retooled its Liberty Ale a few years later to incorporate Cascade hops and came in at forty-seven IBUs. At the time, the average light-lager sported fifteen IBUs, craft breweries were still focused on gateway beers and most beer drinkers ordered their beverage by color: amber, blond, brown and red.

It would take another two decades for IPA to go from curio to king. Back in Boulder County, most brewers point to Gordon Knight as the brewer who kicked open the door for hoppy ales. Avery wasn't far behind, nor was Dale Katechis of Oskar Blues.

But the 1990s were still laying the foundation for a hop explosion. When Avery brewed his generically named India Pale Ale in 1996, P. Ballantine and Sons Brewery, owned by the Pabst Brewing Company, discontinued its own. Founded in 1840 in Newark, New Jersey, Ballantine had been making strong, hoppy ales for decades, but the legacy brand wasn't faring any better than the young Avery.

The tides were changing. The GABF introduced the India Pale Ale category in 1989—Anchor's Liberty Ale took silver—but everything changed in 2000. GABF renamed the category American-Style India Pale Ale and welcomed 89 competitors, second only to the number of entries for American-Style Pale Ale, with 104. In 2001, the entry number rose to 98, and in 2002, the number dropped to 94 but became the most-entered category of the competition—an honor it would hold for GABFs to follow.

Medals aside, hoppy IPAs became a life force for breweries in the twenty-first century. They drew attention from curious drinkers and competition from other breweries. It's no coincidence that the breweries that embraced hops the most also happened to be the breweries that saw the most success.

the Demons of Ale series—weighing in at a whopping 15 percent alcohol by volume. Mephistopheles' Stout followed in 2005, and Samael's Ale (a barleywine) concluded the triumvirate in 2006. Ten years before, any beer north of 8 percent alcohol was considered "big." By the mid-2000s, Avery had three brews north of 15 percent, a healthy roster of ales nipping at their heels and a devout following of beer drinkers just as eager to explore what beer could be as Avery was.

"Beer is just a part of this artisanal movement," Avery said. "I felt my job was to bring wine and spirits people into the beer fold…producing super flavor-forward beers that kind of hit the upper edge of like what beer should be. So that we can have this taste experience that a lot of people want to have, but didn't think was available in beer, because they were thinking of beer as being a ubiquitous kind of lager."

"Not Everybody Survived."

"Whether it was the liquor stores, whether it was the consumer, the restaurants—we were really lucky in those early days," Bob Baile of Twisted Pine Brewing Company said. "Now, some of us didn't make the best business decisions….Not everybody survived; others managed to go gangbusters."

Avery was going gangbusters, Rockies Brewing Company was going gangbusters, Mountain Sun Pub & Brewery was going gangbusters. And George Hanna was getting out.

"It got [to be] more than I wanted to do, and the market was really leveling off," Hanna said. "I thought, 'Boy, this is time to get out.' So, I sold everything I could."

The early 1990s were good to Hanna. The Oasis Brewers Pub was a success, enough to expand and build a twelve-thousand-square-foot production facility in late 1994. The brewing annex, as Hanna dubbed it, was humming, cranking out ten thousand barrels a year. And that included out-of-state distribution.

Oasis had "eight or nine other states by the end of '99," Hanna said. "That's when I really started getting kind of burnt out on everything." Hanna was a restaurateur at heart, but now he was in charge of a package brewery and traveling to Illinois, Texas and Wyoming to set up accounts. Hanna admitted that a good part of his drive was ego—a desire to compete with breweries like Avery, Left Hand and Odell.

"We were holding our own there, but we were still kind of behind the eight ball," Hanna said. "We came from a brewpub, which is really a restaurant and a brewery."

Despite what it might look like on the surface, beer isn't beer isn't beer. Brewing beer is one thing. Selling it is another. Packaging and distributing is another matter altogether. And, as Hanna said, it "took up a lot more time and effort."

"It was really going in a direction that I didn't have my heart in," he said. So, he closed up shop. The Annex ceased production in 2001, and the brewpub followed suit in 2002. Hanna was out, and Baile was in a pickle.

"Shit, now what I'm going to do?" Baile said. Baile's Twisted Pine brewery on Valmont was a small operation. "We had nothing," he said. "I had a little front room, I had three beers on tap, and you could get growlers. That was it."

Baile relied on the Oasis Annex to bottle Twisted Pine beer. Now, he needed to find another facility to contract with. The answer was H.C. Berger Brewing Company in Fort Collins. But a year later, H.C. Berger also sold the business. Again, Baile had to scramble. Then, one day while trying to figure out what to do, Baile drove past the former Oasis Annex at 3201 Walnut Street. "The place was totally empty," Baile said. "Oasis had upgraded all the electrical, all the gas, all the water, and they had put these floors in. And these are high-density concrete floors. I saved $150,000 by moving into this building."[15]

Baile moved Twisted Pine in October 2003. The incestuousness of brewing in Boulder County had extended beyond equipment—now, locations were up for grabs.[16]

CRAFTING FUN

In 2001, Ian Blackford sold his half of Mountain Sun Pub & Brewery, and Kevin Daly went looking for another partner. He didn't have to go far.

"I asked Dad if he wanted to be a silent partner," Daly told the *Daily Camera* in 2009. Sure, the recently retired Tom Daly responded. But he wanted to work.

"I was bored to death," Tom told the *Camera*.

Their first task was to find a second location. Business was crazy at Mountain Sun, and the cramped brewery could only produce so much. The answer was a space three times bigger in a shopping mall located across town on the south side of Broadway. Aptly named, Southern Sun Pub & Brewery opened in September 2002.

"That first expansion was just a stressful time for all of us—trying to expand the original Mountain Sun concept with a full cross-training of the kitchen and the floor," Mountain Sun employee John Fiorilli said. Unlike most restaurants, Mountain Sun didn't differentiate between the front of the house (serving/bartending) and the back of the house (cooking). A Mountain Sun employee could be tossing fries one day and supplying samplers the next. Additionally, employees pooled their tips, distributing them with egalitarian élan. It worked wonders at Mountain Sun. But Southern Sun was three times bigger and with that much more staff. As Fiorilli said, "It was burning all of us out."

Fiorilli left the Mountain Sun family following the opening of Southern Sun (he wouldn't stay away long), and Paul Nashak, who had started working at Mountain Sun in 1995, stepped in as general manager.

Mountain Sun's southern expansion helped alleviate the crush of customers at Mountain Sun, but the facility still had a limitation: it was located on the second level of a shopping center. Weight restrictions prohibited the Dalys from building the brewery out to capacity. They had to settle for a ten-barrel brewhouse inside Southern Sun and resumed the search for a third space, this one capable of a much larger brewing system. That they would find in April 2008, twenty-six miles southeast in Denver, and it was big enough to attract Fiorilli back to the family, this time as the director of brewing operations.

"Been There, Done That."

The 2000s were a good time to be in the brewing business. Despite coming off one of the industry's biggest shakeups and shakeouts, sales and production in the craft sector grew every year.

In the county, two Suns had risen and were shining bright. When Baile's Twisted Pine moved into the old Oasis Annex in 2004, it only took up half of the building's twelve thousand square feet. Within ten years, it would fill it all. And Avery's alley brewery on East Arapahoe Avenue was quickly swallowing adjacent warehouse spaces. Avery's "hobby gone berserk" generated so much demand that the brewery was struggling to keep up. Distribution outside of Colorado was pulled back, and brewers brewed around the clock to keep shelves full and taps pouring.

One of those brewers, Tom Boogaard, left Avery to start his own brewery in Nederland—the first brewery in town since Knight's Wolf Tongue closed in 2001—Wild Mountain Smokehouse & Brewery, founded in 2006.

The *New Brewer* annual industry review issue, 2007. *Courtesy Brewers Association.*

Back at Colorado's first craft brewery, things weren't looking so good. It was time for a change. "We needed to go back to our roots," Jeff Brown said. In 1999, Rockies Brewing sold nineteen thousand barrels of beer. By 2002, it was down to fifteen thousand barrels. Four years of declining sales were enough, and Rockies Brewing needed to change the narrative. Brown was appointed president, and marketing director Dan Weitz joined the team.

A Fort Collins native, Weitz came to Boulder via Odell Brewing Co. Just a few years before, Weitz was sitting in an Old Chicago drinking 90 Shilling—Odell's flagship beer—when he looked up and saw a massive side panel of a truck nailed to the wall. It was advertising New Belgium's Fat Tire. "And I thought to myself, Fat Tire is not as good as 90 Shilling," Weitz said. "I need to talk to the Odell people."

Like the trailblazing brewers who sought to introduce new flavors and beer styles to the marketplace, Weitz had to invent his position, more or less. He bought books about beer and convened with a friend who was BMW's marketing director. He wrote up a plan for Odell and made a job for himself.

"Brought 'em up about 35 percent growth in a couple of years," Weitz said. "We parted ways, and I came to Boulder." In 2002, Odell was up 15 percent over the previous year on a reported twenty-three thousand barrels. By comparison, Rockies Brewing was down 10 percent from the previous year's sales on a reported sixteen thousand barrels.

"We had gone down about four years in a row," Weitz recalled. "But in 2002, 2003, 2004, we started a steady growth up." The main reason: marketing.

"In the old days, you didn't really need it as much because people were clamoring for your product, and there was not much selection," Weitz explained. But as the market became crowded with more and more products, "we had to figure out a way to separate ourselves and what makes us unique and what makes us special."

What made the company special was its longevity. It was the first craft brewery in Colorado, and that meant something. Sure, the name "Rockies Brewing" invoked purple mountains majesty, maybe even a baseball team, but it was also generic. Boulder was specific. It was a place, and as Brown realized, the equity and cachet of the brewery lay not in its broad, regional appeal but in the city's specificity and the brewery's legacy.

So, in 2005, Rockies Brewing Co. became Boulder Beer Co. once more. That year, the brewery reported a 10 percent growth over the previous year and brewed almost eighteen thousand barrels. By decade's end, production would increase to twenty-four thousand barrels.

Management and marketing had a hand to play in the turnaround, as did the beer, particularly Hazed & Infused, a dry-hopped amber ale a decade ahead of its time. "Sometimes we're way too far in front," Weitz said. "Hazed & Infused came out in 2002, and hazy IPAs weren't popular until 2016."

If Boulder Beer's greatest assets were its longevity and legacy, they were also its heaviest handcuffs. Weitz likened it to climbing mountains—by the time you get to the summit, "Boulder Beer isn't there, but our flag is, and we've moved on to the next mountain.

"Been there, done that. Sometimes it sticks, sometimes it doesn't," Weitz said. "We came out with Singletrack in the mid-'90s, and there was another beer, at the same time in Fort Collins that had a bike theme that had a better marketing plan. So, that one resonated better than Singletrack, but Singletrack still was a great beer for about fifteen years. Sometimes you hit it, sometimes you don't."

Sometimes you hit it just enough. Singletrack might have played second fiddle to Fat Tire, but it did what it needed to do for Boulder Beer. Hazed

& Infused did not set the beer world ablaze with the haze craze, but it did become the brewery's top seller in eleven months and kicked off a line of hop-centric ales under the Through the Looking Glass series. But, unlike Ugly Ale and Sport from the 1980s, Through the Looking Glass was in line both with what consumers wanted to drink and what brewers wanted to make. Boulder Beer was getting back to its roots—even back to David Hummer and Randolph Ware's initial conspiracy.

"When we started at the goat shed, we had no idea we wanted to start a business," Ware said. "It was, 'Hey, we want to brew beer.'" And according to Ware, they made every mistake in the book while wanting to brew beer. They also made enough right decisions to last.

"We had no dream that this would be this popular," Ware said during the thirtieth-anniversary celebration of the brewery in 2009. "I guess it worked out well."

"YOU BETTER MAKE THIS FLY."

In 2008, U.S. craft brewing grew by nearly 6 percent—half of the growth rate of 2006 and 2007, but amid the great recession, it was nothing to shake a stick at. "Even when the global meltdown took a bad economy and spiraled it down fast in the fall of 2008, craft brewer sales largely stayed in that low-mid single-digit growth range," Paul Gatza wrote in the 2009 *New Brewer* industry review.

The economy was struggling, but breweries in Boulder were flourishing. Avery Brewing was up 21 percent over the previous year with almost sixteen thousand barrels, Mountain Sun was up 7 percent on thirteen hundred barrels (Southern Sun added another eighteen hundred barrels) and Boulder Beer was up 1 percent on twenty-six thousand barrels.

But entrants to the scene were nonexistent. Except for Republic of Boulder—which came and went in less than twenty-four months—the city of Boulder welcomed no new start-ups.

That changed the first week of November 2008, when Matt Cutter opened the doors to the Upslope Brewing Company at 1501 Lee Hill Drive in North Boulder.

"We had one beer on tap: Upslope Pale Ale," Cutter said. "A smattering of people found the place."

Cutter came to Colorado from Cleveland, Ohio, for skiing, "pure and simple." He graduated from Miami University in 1991 with a major in

Opening day at Upslope Brewing Co. (*Right to left on the brew deck*) Dany Page, Matt Cutter and Henry Wood. *Courtesy Upslope Brewing Company.*

business psychology and then backpacked through Europe for three months but couldn't decide what to do next. A recession was on, and though economic growth returned by June 1992, employment had not. Cutter called a former roommate: Hadn't they talked about moving to Colorado before? Why not now? Nothing was standing in their way—except for jobs. It was summer, and the mountain towns weren't hiring.

"So, by default, we came to Boulder," Cutter said. "We rolled into Boulder, August of 1991. No job, no place to live."

In a few months, the slopes would be open, so they stuck to their initial plan: ski days and work nights. Cutter got a job cooking at Garcia's Mexican Restaurant and met Laura Heinselman, his future wife. She was bartending at Garcia's and down the street at Old Chicago, which pretty much made Cutter an Old Chicago regular. And with 110 beer options to keep him occupied while Heinselman worked, Cutter found his future. "I didn't know beer could taste like that," he said.

Old Chicago's influence went well beyond the beer served. In the early 1990s, Old Chicago was a veritable hotspot for the future of the craft beer industry in Boulder County. Dale Katechis was Laura's bar back, and Kevin Daly was waiting tables. Another regular, Brian Lutz, gathered everyone for parties, at which he served nothing but homebrew. His homebrew got Cutter homebrewing, too, and soon enough, Cutter found his way to South Boulder's on-premise brewing facility, the Beer Store.

"It was a chain out of Canada," Cutter explained. "You'd walk into the store, there would be the kettles right there, they'd have recipes if you wanted to use their recipes, they would have all the ingredients, or you could bring your own, and you would actually brew it there....They would keg it up and carbonate it for you, and then you'd go in and bottle it on-site."

Cutter caught the brewing bug, moving from store to stove. He hooked up with Rico Kellogg, and the two always had beer in the pipeline. It was decent, though "it wasn't flooring anybody," Cutter said. "But it was so fun to discover different styles at the time."

And like a lot of homebrewers, after one too many homebrews, Cutter's mind began to consider the possibilities of a career in beer. In 1996, he took a single semester class on entrepreneurship at Front Range Community College. "The entire semester was putting together a business plan," Cutter said. "People were putting together business plans for flower shops, for software companies and all this, and mine was for a microbrewery."

Dubbed New World Brewing, Cutter showed the plan to friends, primarily brewers, particularly Lutz and Dave Watson, who were brewing at Left Hand Brewing Company.[17] Watson was curious and looked for locations with Cutter, but nothing came of it.

"Nobody had any money," Cutter said. "We were young and broke. I started having kids the following year. So, we shelved it." Cutter went into project management in the tech industry. Oddly enough, the next ten years of start-up groundwork and understanding the manufacturing process did more to help Cutter establish a successful brewery than eking out a living while trying to keep a brewery afloat for a decade.

"I love that we would take raw materials, put them through a process—a manufacturing process—and, at the end of the day, there were tangible finished goods sitting in the shipping area," Cutter said. "That was very satisfying to me."

In 1998, Cutter joined Seagate Technology in Longmont. Next came IBM in Boulder. All the while, he thought, what if? Cutter kept homebrewing and kept dreaming of the brewery. In 2007, he decided to dust off the old New World Brewing plan and see what could be done with it. For a lot of dreamers, nothing would have come of it. Cutter could have have looked at it, entertained the idea for a month or a year and then gone back to the day job and family. But that's not how this story was to play out. At the crucial moment, Cutter's ten-year-old son, Gabe, intervened.

"I remember Gabe coming to me and being like, 'Dad, what are you doing?'" Cutter said. "I'm just like, 'Oh, I'm writing a business plan.' 'For what?' 'Well, it's for a microbrewery, but you should be getting to bed.'

"I was trying to tell him that it was just an exercise at the time, and he was just like, 'A microbrewery? Yeah, you have to do that. It's your dream.'"

Yeah, Cutter thought, why wouldn't I do that? It's my dream. In January 2008, Cutter became a "homebrewer with a business plan."

But Cutter hadn't brewed on anything larger than a five-gallon carboy. He needed a professional brewer. And there was one, seven thousand miles south, who needed a brewery in Colorado to call home.

Much like the guys from Boulder Brewing starting their first brewery in a goat shed, Dany Page began in a chicken coop behind his rental house in Ushuaia, Argentina, in 2000. Located on an outpost in Tierra del Fuego, Beagle Brewery (named after the Beagle Channel, itself named after Charles Darwin's research ship, the HMS *Beagle*) was the world's southernmost

Upslope's cofounder and brewer Dany Page. *Courtesy Upslope Brewing Company.*

brewery and had the first tap handle on Antarctica—at the Spanish research station, Gabriel de Castilla Base. The brewery was humble and produced about eight hundred barrels of beer in eight hundred square feet of space from handmade tanks built by a local welder.

Then, in the summer of 2007, one of Page's friends rented a room to a teacher from Aurora, Colorado (a suburb of Denver), who was on an exchange program. Like Cutter falling for Laura at Garcia's and subsequently following her to Old Chicago, Page fell for the teacher and followed her back to Colorado. He needed a job, and Cutter needed a brewer. Cutter put out an ad, and Page answered. The two met at a coffee shop in North Boulder and discussed what they envisioned in a brewery. Coincidentally, they both wanted to can their beers.

"It was all about the active outdoor enthusiast craft beer drinker," Cutter said. "And the best vessel for that demographic is a can. That was the whole thing—the portability of the can."

Now they needed space. Cutter found a 2,700-square-foot unit in North Boulder's Lee Hill neighborhood and signed a one-year lease. Page vacated his Argentine apartment, sold his car and left Beagle Brewing to his partners. Colorado called.

"He could not believe how mature Colorado was," Cutter explained, "in terms of the number of craft breweries, people seeking out craft beer….Not to mention access to raw materials: malt, hops, yeast, access to equipment," all of which Page struggled to find in Argentina. But struggle cultivates creativity, and Page brought plenty to the brewery. Combine that with access to materials and a public clamoring for good beer, and Cutter and Page were bound to succeed—as long as the money held out.

"You better make this fly," Leslie told Cutter as they took out a second mortgage on their house.

THE TYRANNY OF FAST GROWTH

Between the beginning of November and the end of December 2008, Upslope Brewing Company brewed eighty barrels of beer.[18] Not bad, Cutter recalled, but one anxiety led to another.

"Henry was putting a lot of pressure on us to get things dialed in by early November," he said. Henry was Henry Wood, a dirtbag climber from Atlanta, Georgia, spearheading Upslope's marketing and sales. Wood had

Dany Page, Henry Wood and Matt Cutter tap Upslope's first keg of Pale Ale. *Courtesy Upslope Brewing Company.*

a simple sales plan: empty cold room. He would sell every last can of Upslope beer.

"He did that for about three years," Cutter said. And he did it even before the beer was brewed, visiting area liquor stores with a picture of a can of beer to see how receptive retailers would be to a new brewery.

Wood sold every last drop, and retailers ordered more. But Cutter was broke. By February 2009, Upslope was out of money. Worse, the great recession locked down lending, and every bank in the area turned Cutter down. His only resort was to refinance his first mortgage with the second and pull more money out of his house.

"It was so difficult because we were growing so quickly," Cutter said. "It was, 'Ah! You're growing fast, that's great!' Well, it's great from a sales perspective, but from a cash flow perspective, it is brutal. Because everything you've produced and sold finally gets paid for and has to go right back into the business to fuel all of that growth."

Whether it is raw materials needed, equipment or physical space, production costs eat up roughly two-thirds of a brewery's sales. As Cutter explained, one tap handle at a bar or restaurant could tie up hundreds of dollars of beer and equipment: "You need a keg that's on the line, you need a keg in the cooler and then there's an empty keg in their cage in the back alley, and then you have to have their next [on the way]. So, you have to have at least four kegs to service one tap handle. That's a lot of kegs."

Many breweries had fallen to similar fates. Tony Magee of Lagunitas Brewing Company would call it the "tyranny of fast growth," and the tyranny sank more than one brewery.

But then Cutter was thrown a lifeline. An agent from one of the banks that turned Cutter down had relocated to a credit union and saw something she liked in Cutter's business plan. She extended Cutter a $10,000 line of credit, "and I am screaming victory," Cutter says. "I got a loan from the bank!"

The timing couldn't have been better. Upslope needed more tanks, and Cutter had to replace the filter and fix the cooler. That's fine, the credit union said, here's more. Slowly but surely, a safety net was sewn beneath Cutter's feet. "My original business projected 450 barrels that we would do in 2009," Cutter said. "When Henry started selling, we adjusted that up to 650 barrels. And in that first year, we produced and sold 1,100 barrels of beer."

And those eleven hundred barrels were two beers: Pale Ale and India Pale Ale. The latter was the first IPA in the state to be canned and became Upslope's number-one seller. Two years later, a third followed, Brown Ale, and then a fourth, Craft Lager. Upslope's "core four" was set.

"The screws were falling off the walls," Cutter said. They were brewing beer nonstop six days a week. In 2012, "we produced and sold 5,600 barrels. On a 7-barrel brewhouse," Cutter said—eight hundred brews in a single year, or an average of two brews a day. Cutter started looking for a second space.

The 1981 American Homebrewers Association National Homebrewers Conference post-conference gathering at the original Boulder Brewing Company. (*Front row, left to right*): Michael Jackson, Otto Zavatone and Fred Eckhardt. (*Second row, left to right*): Charlie Papazian, Alvin Nelson, Al Andrews and Tom Burns. (*Back Row, left to right*): Steve Gering and Lee Damkoehler. *Photo by Weldon Gregg, courtesy Boulder Beer Co.*

Jeff Brown and David Zuckerman. *Courtesy Boulder Beer Co.*

Above: Twenty-two-ounce bomber of Hog Heaven Dry-Hopped Barleywine-style ale. *Courtesy Avery Brewing Co.*

Right: Dan Weitz. *Courtesy Boulder Beer Co.*

The core four. *Courtesy Upslope Brewing Co.*

David Hummer, Randolph Ware and Alvin Nelson returning from a junkyard run with equipment for the brewery at the goat shed. *Courtesy Boulder Beer Co.*

Aaron Stueck of BJ's Restaurant & Brewhouse. *Author photo.*

Pumphouse Brewery's Red Alert Amber. *Author photo.*

The back entrance of Pumphouse Restaurant & Brewery is lined with empty beer bottles from all over. *Author photo.*

Larry and Adam Avery inside the brewery on Arapahoe Avenue, circa 2014. *Courtesy Avery Brewing Co.*

Cans of Dale's Pale Ale, circa 2002. *Courtesy Oskar Blues Brewery.*

Wibby Brewing's Lightshine Helles. *Author photo.*

A pint of Shoes & Brews' Frankly My Dear I Don't Guava Damn Pale Ale. *Author photo.*

Gravity Brewing's Acceleration Double IPA. *Author photo.*

A sampler display of the more than one hundred varieties of malt extracts and beer kits from which a homebrewer may choose. *Courtesy Charlie Papazian, taken for his book* The Complete Joy of Homebrewing.

Boulder Brewing Company, circa 1984. *Courtesy of Boulder Beer Co.*

Charlie Papazian, circa 1970s. *Courtesy Brewers Association.*

Left: American Homebrewers Association coaster. *Courtesy Division of Work and Industry, National Museum of American History, Smithsonian Institution.*

Below: Interior of BJ's Restaurants & Brewhouse on Pearl Street. *Courtesy Alex Puchner.*

Greg Kallfa and Adam Kandle of Boulder Fermentation Supply and Vision Quest Brewing. *Author photo.*

Brewer Brian Lutz of RedFish New Orleans Brewhouse, Left Hand Brewing Company, Oskar Blues Brewery and West Flanders Brewing Co. *Courtesy West Flanders Brewing Co.*

Twisted Pine Brewing Company's kettle and mash tun. *Author photo.*

Avery Brewing's Holy Trinity of Ales. *Courtesy Avery Brewing Co.*

Avery Brewing's award-winning barrel age series. *Courtesy of Avery Brewing Co.*

Canning at Crystal Springs Brewing Company on a Wild Goose system. *Author photo.*

Hazy IPAs at Odd13 Brewing. *Author photo.*

Adam Avery at the taproom on Arapahoe Avenue. *Courtesy Avery Brewing Co.*

Tasters at West Flanders Brewing Co. *Author photo.*

Oskar Blues Brewery's Tasty Weasel taproom and production brewery. *Courtesy Oskar Blues Brewery.*

Left Hand Brewing Co. cofounder Eric Wallace, circa 2015. *Courtesy Left Hand Brewing Co.*

5
PURSUIT AS HAPPINESS

The Third Generation

Boulder Brewing's David Hummer and Randolph Ware were among the first generation of craft brewers—a small, nationwide group looking to drink something other than everyday, mass-market lagers. The second generation grew up drinking the first's beer, and regardless of what beer it was, the refrain was always the same: "I didn't know beer could taste like that." If the first generation cleared the metaphorical landscape, built the foundation and applied for permits, then the second generation erected the house.

Like most industries, brewing is a group effort. Developments play off of each other, and advancements are incremental. When Hummer and Ware built their brewery in 1979, all of their equipment was obtained secondhand and repurposed. Three decades later, future brewers could order whole systems, designed to personal specifications, from the comfort of their home—ditto for raw materials, financing and acceptance. When Boulder Brewing first bottled its bitter, porter and stout in 1980, they were described as "big beers" because of their full-bodied malt flavor and hop aroma. Then, in 2004, Avery Brewing Co. released the Beast Grand Cru and reconfigured the notion of what a big beer is or could be.

The craft beer palate had shifted.

CRAFT CATCHES FIRE

But it wasn't just drinkers' palates that changed; the business of craft brewing had markedly shifted. In the second decade of the twenty-first century, small and local businesses also saw a seismic shift, namely in the capital that was easier to come by, accessibility to equipment and raw materials and a public that was becoming more prolific and more promiscuous. By the end of 2010, eleven breweries and brewpubs operated in Boulder city limits. A dozen more would open in the next five years. These breweries were smaller than their predecessors, revolved primarily around the taproom model and produced barrels in the low hundreds. Most of the beer was sold and consumed on-site, and the sheer number of breweries turned the city's brewing culture into a tourist destination.

Not all were successes. When the RedFish New Orleans Brewhouse closed in January 2009, the 2027 Thirteenth Street location became a revolving door for brewpubs. Jim Howser and Mitch Arden bought the space and opened the Boulder Draft House on Valentine's Day 2009. They brought out Chicago brewer Mike Kasian to brew the beer, under the name Colorado Brewing Company, but neither could swing. The Boulder Draft House closed on December 31, 2010.

Next up was Los Oasis Latin Grill & Cerveceria—George Hanna's attempt to resurrect the Oasis concept and pair it with high-end Mexican plates. Kasian came with the building but didn't brew long. Hanna's business partner was financing the whole shebang but couldn't keep the funding long enough to build any traction. Los Oasis lived for roughly six months, June 2011 to November 2011, before turning over the keys.

Enter the Emich triplets—Jessica, Jill and Jennifer—who rebranded the space as the Shine Restaurant & Gathering Place in December 2011. Two months later, Kasian got the brewery portion up and running. For six years, Shine found a fair amount of success, but in September 2017, the Emich sisters ditched the digs and the brewing and moved their Shine concept to a shopping mall a mile east. Two months later, the Post Brewing Co. stepped in and became the fifth brewery to call 2027 Thirteenth Street home.

Shine's concept took an organic and gluten-free approach to the menu, an attitude Kasian also employed in the brewing process, which extended the craft beer olive branch to a large number of health-conscious and gluten-intolerant drinkers.

Kasian was not alone. Pedro Gonzalez found out he was gluten-intolerant in 2003 but resolved not to let it end his beer-drinking days. When he discovered gluten-free beers in the market, he asked a friend to show him how to brew. And in 2009, Gonzalez debuted New Planet Beer—Boulder's first gluten-free brewery.

Chris Asher wasn't far behind. In November 2009, he opened Asher Brewing Company, Boulder's first all-organic brewery. Before his namesake brewery, Asher brewed at RedFish, where he unveiled his first organic IPA. The beer became a bestseller at the brewpub, and ten months after RedFish closed up shop, Asher opened his own, the first brewery in Gunbarrel at 4669 Nautilus Court. Located ten miles northeast of Boulder, Gunbarrel seemed like a far cry from the Boulder city hotbed of breweries, but within five years, Asher would have an impressive neighbor—drawing plenty of beer enthusiasts with it.

Asher Brewing wasn't the only brewery to extend the Boulder brewing hub off Pearl Street. In June 2013, BRU handbuilt ales & eats opened the doors to its East Boulder brewpub after its genesis in Ian Clark's North Boulder garage one year before.

BRU (the name is the airport code from Brussels, Belgium) was the product of hard work, homebrew and the husband-and-wife team of Ian and Bryce Clark. Less than half a mile away, another husband-and-wife team, Jake and Erin Evans, opened Wild Woods Brewing Co. in September 2012. Originally from Wisconsin, the couple relocated to Boulder in 2007, when Jake got a job as an electrical engineer. They shared a love for the mountains and a taste for full-flavored beer. Soon, the two merged, and the combination of Jake's homebrew around the campfire proved to be intoxicating. A plan was hatched, and they partnered with another couple, Charlie and Kristen Rilling.

Located in an office park reminiscent of a series of warehouse garages, Wild Woods adhered to an industrial atmosphere with minimal accouterments—high-top bar, a handful of tables, light stainless steel chairs and sparse décor reflecting the brand. In the coming years, more brewers would look like Wild Woods than not. These breweries would also be on the small side. Wild Woods started on a two-barrel system (it would upgrade to seven barrels in the future). Two miles east in the East Pearl Business Park, Jamie Wells opened his brewery, J. Wells Brewery, in January 2013 on a one-and-a-half-barrel system.

Not far from Wild Woods, Upslope Brewing Company took over a warehouse in Flatiron Park, a large business campus. The building was one of nineteen that had been acquired by Crescent Real Estate, and the group wanted a brewery in the neighborhood.

Upslope's three conical fermenters arrive at Flatiron Park in 2012. *Courtesy Upslope Brewing Company.*

"They had approached Adam Avery, and Adam was like, 'No, no, I got other stuff going on,'" Matt Cutter said. "So, we show up, and they're like, 'So, you're a brewery.'" That was in the summer of 2012. On February 9, 2013, Cutter and company fired up the brewhouse and brewed a batch of pale ale.

"We started with three 120-barrel fermenters and a 30-barrel brewhouse," Cutter said. "We were scared shitless."

The gamble paid off. That year, Upslope produced and sold over eleven thousand barrels of beer. "It was a rocketship," Cutter said.

Back in Gunbarrel, Eric Huber—a former brewer at Mountain Sun and Oskar Blues—gathered his cousin and neighbor to open the Kettle & Stone Brewing Company in June 2013, with a ten-barrel brewhouse and designs to produce can-conditioned and bottle-conditioned beer for distribution. But when Stone Brewing in California threatened a cease-and-desist order over the name four months later, Huber changed it to Vindication Brewing Company to avoid litigation. That was in the spring of 2014, just a few months before Finkel & Garf Brewing Company moved into the area.

Breweries were popping up two at a time. Not far from Boulder Beer, and a few blocks from J. Wells, Adam Kandle and Greg Kallfa expanded their homebrew shop, Boulder Fermentation Supply, to incorporate a taproom, Vision Quest Brewing Company, in August 2015. In September 2013, half a mile away, two former Boulder Beer employees, Michael Memsic and Chris

Coyne, partnered with Zach Nichols to open Sanitas Brewing Co. It was the fourth brewery to open in the city that year.

Much like Kettle & Stone/Vindication, Sanitas Brewing's business plan involved distribution. It came out of the gate swinging with two canned offerings: Black IPA and Saison—the first canned saison in Colorado.

With so many breweries opening in quick succession, it's easy to find commonalities between them. But commonalities also reduce individuality, and beyond the simple fact that they made beer, there's not a lot that J. Wells and Sanitas had in common. The same can be said for FATE Brewing Company, a start-up brewpub that tried to compress the success and growth Mountain Sun saw in a decade down by half. FATE opened its doors in February 2013 and rode the craft beer wave as long as possible, but after five years, the wheels started coming off.

In the early 1990s, it seemed like a brewpub couldn't miss. That wasn't the case in the 2010s. To make it, you had to play your cards a little bit closer to the vest. BJ's Restaurant & Brewhouse had done wonders on Pearl Street, but the brewing setup was far from ideal. It was much easier to brew BJ's beer at a production facility and then distribute it back at the stores.

In 2006, BJ's opened a brewpub in Reno, Nevada, capable of producing fifteen thousand barrels of beer annually. And with BJ's core lineup of

Sanitas Brewing Company's Chris Coyne, Michael Memsic and Zach Nichols pose in front of cans of Black IPA. *Courtesy Sanitas Brewing Company.*

beers brewed elsewhere, the Pearl Street location was free to try something different, something new—something to satisfy the Boulder palate, as brewer Aaron Stueck said.

Stueck started brewing with BJ's on Pearl Street. When the company vacated its location in 2012 for a new building located in the Twenty-Ninth Street mall (a collection of trendy shops and eateries), Stueck was promoted to head the research and development division. Essentially, Stueck got to play with flavors, ingredients and processes. If his three-barrel R&D brewhouse could handle it, he could do it. And if the beer sold in Boulder, BJ's would consider it for production on a nationwide scale.

Like 2027 Thirteenth Street, BJ's 1125 Pearl Street brewpub didn't stay empty long. In September 2012, owners Chris and Mark Heinritz and brewer Brian Lutz returned to downtown Boulder with a concept that played to Lutz's brewing strengths: West Flanders Brewing Co., a Belgian-inspired brewpub.

A THIRD NATION, A THIRD INSPIRATION

No other nation has a more colorful, individualist, or idiosyncratic assortment of beers.
—*Michael Jackson,* The New World Guide to Beer

Brian Lutz debuted his Angry Monk—then called Trappist-style ale—at the RedFish New Orleans Brewhouse in 1996. Drinkers in Boulder had no time for it.[19] But by the time West Flanders Brewing Company opened in 2012, Boulder drinkers had caught up to Angry Monk.

For more than a century, Americans drank German-inspired lagers in a tradition brought over during the nineteenth century by brewers like Phillip Best, Frederick Pabst, Adolphus Busch and Adolph Coors. They introduced thirsty Americans to bright golden beers, and their wares became the dominant beer style. Many craft brewers tried their hand at the same and succeeded, but in the early days of the craft beer revolution, their bread and butter were English-inspired ales: pales, porters, stouts and the like. Then, in the twenty-first century, styles and techniques from a third brewing nation invaded America: Belgium.

In 2006, Sam Calagione of Delaware's Dogfish Head Craft Brewery was at work on a book, *Extreme Homebrewing: An Introduction to Brewing Craft Beer at Home*, when it became clear that to truly understand extreme brewing, he would have to see with his own eyes, smell with his own nose and taste with his own mouth the Belgian way of brewing. "I knew this book would be incomplete without a pilgrimage to the motherland of extreme brewing," Calagione wrote in the *New Brewer.*

Eager to share the wealth, Calagione invited four close friends and like-minded brewers, Tomme Arthur of Port Brewing/Lost Abbey, Rob Tod of Allagash Brewing Company, Vinnie Cilurzo of Russian River Brewing Company and Adam Avery of Avery Brewing Co. The "Brett Pack" was off.[20]

After a whirlwind five days of beer in Belgium, Avery returned with a thirst for sour beer. The brewery started experimenting with a koelschip (pronounced "cool ship," a large shallow tub where hot wort is cooled and spontaneously fermented with airborne microorganisms), mimicking what he saw at Brasserie Cantillon, and using wine barrels inoculated with Brettanomyces yeast harvested from Drie Fonteinen.[21]

In the 1990s, Avery couldn't sell a bitter beer if his life depended on it. Then drinkers caught up, and Avery's India pale ale became the brewery's number-one seller. In 2003, Avery introduced White Rascal Belgian-Style White Ale. Two years later, Rascal became its number-one seller.

The experiments were paying off, but the alley on Arapahoe Avenue could no longer contain the business. In 2009, Avery Brewing surpassed fifteen thousand barrels, moving it from the micro category to regional. By 2015, it would almost scratch fifty thousand barrels, and it would do so in a brand-new facility.

Tomme Arthur, Vinnie Cilurzo and Adam Avery in Belgium. *Courtesy Avery Brewing Co.*

Groundbreaking cheers at Avery's Gunbarrel brewery, circa 2014. *Courtesy Avery Brewing Co.*

In September 2011, Avery submitted plans for a seventy-two-thousand-square-foot brewery on five and a half acres of land in Gunbarrel, practically across the street from Asher Brewing. The facility would have everything Avery had on Arapahoe—brewery, warehouse and offices—just bigger and better, with the addition of a restaurant and gift shop.

Avery's projected plans for seventy-two thousand square feet shrank to fifty-eight thousand during planning before settling on sixty-seven thousand square feet. Exterior space allowing it to expand to ninety-five thousand square feet—a far cry from the twenty thousand that struggled to contain the brewery on Arapahoe Avenue.

More importantly, Avery's Gunbarrel facility ushered in a new era of brewing in Boulder. In 1984, the guys at Boulder Brewing relocated from a goat shed to their castle-like structure on Wilderness—planting the flag for brewers in Boulder. But over the next three decades, the movement was confined primarily to brewpubs and garages, small taprooms and smaller production. Sporting an 85-barrel brewhouse inside a state-of-the-art facility with four 720-barrel fermenters looming over the complex, Avery was now capable of producing 350,000 barrels of beer a year.

The sky was the limit.

PART II

LONGMONT, LYONS, NEDERLAND AND NIWOT

6

"A DISTURBANCE IN THE FORCE."

Located fifteen miles northeast of Boulder and founded in 1871 by the Chicago-Colorado Colony, Longmont was the true birthplace of craft brewing in Colorado. When the Bureau of Alcohol, Tobacco and Firearms issued Boulder Brewing Company a permit in 1979, the address it listed was 15555 North Eighty-Third Street, Longmont, Colorado 80501.

Boulder Brewing moved south to its namesake in 1984. It would be another decade before Longmont started producing beer again, but one brewery would give way to many. By 2015, two of those would be among the most influential in the entire craft beer movement.

"Now Is the Time."

Like many brewing communities, Longmont's beer scene was conceived overseas before taking root on American soil. Eric Wallace and Dick Doore were the first to plant their flag in the town of fifty-one thousand.

Born in Memphis, Tennessee, Wallace was the son of an air force officer and grew up all over the world, notably going to high school in Germany before returning to the States, "confused and flabbergasted that the wealthiest country on Earth had such a monochromatic view of the beer world."

Following in his father's footsteps, Wallace joined the Air Force Academy, then tech school and spent the remainder of the 1980s overseas.

DEPARTMENT OF THE TREASURY
BUREAU OF ALCOHOL, TOBACCO AND FIREARMS
BREWER'S NOTICE
(Prepare in triplicate – see instructions on back)

1. SERIAL NUMBER: 1

2. TO: REGIONAL REGULATORY ADMINISTRATOR, BUREAU OF ALCOHOL, TOBACCO AND FIREARMS *(City and State)*
Dallas, Texas

3. DATE: 1 Feb. 1979

4. THIS NOTICE IS FILED TO SHOW:
[X] ORIGINAL ESTABLISHMENT
[ ] AMENDED OR SUPPLEMENTAL INFORMATION GIVEN IN ITEMS BELOW (Indicate item nos.)
[ ] CONTINUATION OF BUSINESS UNDER NEW BOND OR CONTINUATION CERTIFICATE

5. NAME OF BREWER
David G. Hummer, Alvin D. Nelson
Randolph H. Ware

6. BUSINESS ADDRESS (No., Street, City, State, Zip Code)
15555 N. 83rd St. Longmont, Colo. 80501

7. BREWERY ADDRESS *(If different from business address)*

8. CHARACTER OF BREWER *(Sole proprietorship, partnership, corporation, etc.)*
Partnership

9. DESCRIPTION OF BREWERY *((A) Each tract of land comprising the brewery; (B) Buildings)*
See attached legal description

THIS DOCUMENT SHOULD BE KEPT READILY AVAILABLE FOR INSPECTION BY OFFICERS OF THE BUREAU OF ALCOHOL, TOBACCO, AND FIREARMS.

10. EQUIPMENT FOR PRODUCING BEER *((A) Mash tubs; (B) Brewkettles; (C) Fermenting tanks; (D) Storage tanks; (E) Other similar tanks; (F) Bottling tanks; (G) Bottling lines)*
See attached

This permit (Registration, notice) is conditioned on compliance by you with the purposes of the Federal Water Pollution Control Act (33 U.S.C. 1171(b))

11. TRADE NAMES TO BE USED *(Name, office where registered, how used)*
Boulder Beer, Secretary of State, State of Colorado

12. STATEMENT OF PROCESS *(Fermented beverages produced and marketed under a name or description other than "beer," "ale," "porter," or "stout.")*
See Attached

13. TITLE TO PREMISES
A. D. Nelson, unencumbered owner

14. TITLE TO APPARATUS AND EQUIPMENT
All apparatus and equipment owned by partnership David G. Hummer, Alvin D. Nelson, Randolph H. Ware

15. DETAILS OF OWNERSHIP
Partnership, David G. Hummer, Alvin D. Nelson, Randolph H. Ware

16. DETAILS OF CONTROL AND MANAGEMENT
See Attachment

All data, written statements, affidavits and other documents submitted in support hereof shall be deemed to be part of this notice.
Under penalties of perjury, I declare that I have examined this notice and to the best of my knowledge and belief it is true, correct, and complete.

17. SIGNATURE OF BREWER
David G. Hummer, Alvin D. Nelson, Randolph H. Ware T/A Boulder beer

18. BY *(Name and title)*
Randolph H. Ware [signature] Partner

DEPARTMENT OF THE TREASURY - BUREAU OF ALCOHOL, TOBACCO AND FIREARMS *(City and State)*
Dallas, Texas

DATE: SEP 25 1979

THE FOREGOING NOTICE IS
[ ] NOT APPROVED
[X] APPROVED

EFFECTIVE DATE: SEP 25 1979

SIGNATURE OF REGIONAL REGULATORY ADMINISTRATOR, BUREAU OF ALCOHOL, TOBACCO AND FIREARMS
[signature] for Earl P. Kennard

ATF FORM 27-C (5130.10) (2-77) PREVIOUS EDITIONS ARE OBSOLETE

Above: Boulder Brewing Company's 1979 permit. *Courtesy Boulder Beer Co.*

Opposite: Eric Wallace and Dick Doore pose next to the original Left Hand Brewing sign in 1993. *Courtesy Left Hand Brewing Co.*

It was at the Academy in 1982 that Wallace crossed paths with Doore (born in Kittanning, Pennsylvania, and raised in a rural New Hampshire farm town).

Life overseas—in Germany, Italy, Turkey and England—contributed to their sense of beer-drinking cultures. Both returned to the States in the early 1990s, settled in Niwot (a small town located halfway between Boulder and Longmont) and decided to partner. Wallace was invigorated by a recent cross-country trip of every major craft brewery at the time, from New Orleans, Louisiana, "all the way to Homer, Alaska, and back." Doore, who had just returned from India, had been homebrewing since his brother gave him a kit in 1990. Enthusiasm collided with experience.

"It's finally happening!" Wallace said. "I guess I have a karmic obligation to get involved in this because I've bitched and moaned about it for so long."

So, Wallace went to Doore. "Dude, what are we going to do?" Wallace recounted. "This beer thing is going to happen. Now is the time. It is the time."

According to Doore, the first beer they brewed together was a stout. "We brewed it once. And started drinking that first batch," Doore told Theresa McCulla in 2017. "I think by the end of that evening, we had decided to start a brewery."

The following day, Doore and Wallace hashed out the details. The two visited every brewery they could drive to, talked to any brewer who would give them time and broke down any beer they could drink for inspiration. They also became frequent customers at What's Brewing Homebrew Supply and Liquor Mart, brewing all-grain batches twice a week. That caught the eye of manager Paul Gatza, who would later connect Wallace with Brian Lutz, then bartending at La Estrellita at 2027 Thirteenth Street, Boulder.[22]

Now they needed a place to brew. They made inquiries around the area, and Longmont answered. The city's mayor, Fred Wilson, was a homebrewer and was eager to help them. He suggested a former meatpacking plant located at 1265 Boston Avenue along the St. Vrain Creek. Boulder, on the other hand, didn't call back.

"They were not really interested. Different agenda down there," Wallace told McCulla. "Longmont was very welcoming. Which was probably one of the reasons that we ended up here and the availability of space up here."

And the 5,300-square-foot Green Sausage Factory proved ideal—even if the previous owner, Curtis Green, lost his right arm in a sausage grinder. Oddly enough, that's not where the brewery got the name Left Hand. Wallace and Doore originally wanted to call their brewery Indian Peak Brewing Company, but another brewery had a line of beers with a similar name. So, they looked to their home of Niwot—the Southern Arapaho word for "left hand"—and drew inspiration there.

They also moved fast. One month after they decided to start a brewery, Wallace and Doore incorporated Left Hand Brewing Company on September 21, 1993, started building out the brewery in October and brewed their first batch of beer, Sawtooth Amber Ale, on January 2, 1994.

"We were ready to brew the last few days of December [1993]," Wallace said. "But there was an occupational tax [$500 a year], and it's prorated.

"We were so broke," Wallace continued. "We were so broke, we were like, 'Ah man, we're not going to pay forty-something dollars for a single brew. We'll wait a month.'"

And on January 22, 1994, with "twenty-something dollars in our bank account," the Left Hand Brewing Company opened for business. Wallace and Doore brewed a little over fourteen hundred barrels of beer that

Dick Doore and Eric Wallace pose next to Charlie Papazian after their gold medal win for their Black Jack Porter at the 1995 Great American Beer Festival. *Courtesy Left Hand Brewing Co.*

year and won a gold medal for Sawtooth at the 1994 Great American Beer Festival.

Though Left Hand saw rapid growth from 1994 through 1998, the capital-intensive nature of brewing made for lean times at the brewery. Then, in April 1998, Left Hand bought Tabernash Brewing, a struggling brewery from Denver's River North district. "The first shakeout was on, and breweries were failing left and right," Wallace said. "They were going to go under, so we joined forces."

Leading with a weissbier—Bavaria's wheat beer, also known as hefeweizen outside of Germany—Tabernash was draft only and contract brewing at New Belgium Brewery in Fort Collins. The partnership looked good in spirit, but it cash-strapped Wallace and Doore. "We were managing two different wholesalers, and that wasn't working," Wallace said.

"And then Left Hand's wholesaler tried to put us out," Wallace continued. "They closed down their division and left us hanging."

That was in June, three days before Left Hand planned to ship its first twelve-ounce six-packs. In Wallace's eyes, the timing in his "conspiracy theory mind" was not a coincidence. He concluded that the wholesaler tried to put Left Hand out of business because they would rather have worked

GREAT AMERICAN BEER FESTIVAL

Before the craft beer revolution, the American beer culture was nonexistent. "In those days, the closest thing to a beer fest was a kegger in the woods," Charlie Papazian said.

It's no surprise, then, that so much of what kicked off the movement originated overseas. The Great American Beer Festival (GABF) was no different, and it first started fermenting in Papazian's mind at the Great British Beer Festival (GBBF) in 1981.

First organized in 1977 by the Campaign for Real Ale (CAMRA), GBBF was a celebration and a preservation of unfiltered, unpasteurized, cask-conditioned "real ale," Britain's brewing tradition. For the 1981 iteration, the festival invited Papazian as a judge. His charge: sit on a three-person panel and determine the grand champion beers of England. Recounting the festival years later in *Microbrewed Adventures*, Papazian used the word *awed* to describe his experience.

Following GBBF, Papazian traveled to London and reconnected with friend and British beer scribe Michael Jackson. He talked of people relaxing, drinking traditional ales, talking about flavors and enjoying a beverage the way the brewers intended. "We should do this in America," Papazian told Jackson. "That's a great idea, Charlie," Jackson responded. "Only, what will you serve for beer?"

Jackson had every right to be skeptical. At the time, only forty-four breweries were operating in the United States, and the number was dwindling. Regionals were either consolidating or closing up. But enthusiasm for homebrewing, spurred in great part by Papazian's efforts, foretold the coming revolution.

"By 1981, there was a well-established community, a network, of homebrewers and beer enthusiasts in Boulder and the Denver area," Papazian said. "There were four of us who were the core group who discussed the idea of putting together a beer festival where we could celebrate what was left of American beer because there wasn't a whole lot."

The four were Papazian, Tom Burns (Boulder Brewing's brewmaster) and two students of Papazian's weekly homebrewing class, Frank Morris, a Liquor Mart employee who Papazian cites as "instrumental" for championing imported beer, and Stuart Harris, a software engineer who also wrote for *Zymurgy*, the homebrewing magazine Papazian launched in 1978. Inspired by Papazian's experience at GBBF, the goal was to celebrate and elevate America's rich brewing history.

The 1982 Great American Beer Festival at the Hilton Harvest House Hotel. *Courtesy Brewers Association.*

Coincidentally, CAMRA (and subsequently GBBF) was founded in 1971 by four men fearing ubiquitous bland beers would obliterate British brewing heritage. They aimed to preserve tradition and promote quality. Ten years later, four men in Boulder picked up the baton.

The first GABF was held in a five-thousand-square-foot ballroom inside Boulder's Hilton Harvest House Hotel on Friday, June 4, 1982, the centerpiece event of the fourth annual National Homebrewers and Microbrewery Conference, put on by the American Homebrewers Association. It lasted from 4:30 to 9:30 p.m. During those five hours, forty-seven beers from twenty-four breweries were poured for eight hundred guests.

solely with New Belgium or Odell. Regardless, Wallace found a way to work with the lemons.

"After a bunch of gyrations, we started our own distribution company," he explained. "We'd been self-distributing in Boulder County the whole time. So, using that as the base—as the skeleton—we built onto that and started distributing on a more widespread basis, going all the way down to Denver and into the mountains."

Formed in November, Indian Peaks Distribution Company (never let a good name go unused) partnered with High Point Brewing Corp. in Eagle, Bristol Brewing in Colorado Springs, Ska Brewing in Durango and Avery Brewing in Boulder to create a distribution network among independent, like-minded breweries. And as it expanded, so did its reach, including North Coast Brewing, Anderson Valley Brewing, Dogfish Head Brewery,

Milk Stout and Nitro Milk Stout. *Courtesy Left Hand Brewing Co.*

Stone Brewing, Allagash Brewing, Hair of the Dog Brewing and Two Brothers Artisan Brewing.

"We started bringing all of these brands into Colorado because Colorado was a good beer market—it was independent liquor stores and super competitive and super open," Wallace says.[23] Indian Peaks Distribution "got nominally profitable over about seven years," while Left Hand stayed flat—the norm in the industry at that time.

"In January 2006, we sold our distribution company to C.R. Goodman," Wallace continued. "That allowed us to be debt-free and really focus on building a sales force and trying to grow. And that was the first of ten years of double-digit growth."

It also opened the door for Left Hand's next milestone: Milk Stout. First brewed in 1999, Left Hand's future flagship drew inspiration from a trip to Tanzania, where Doore discovered Castle Stout (a stout dosed with unfermentable milk sugar). That lactose gives the beer a creamy mouth and a dollop of sweetness between dark roasted malts and bitter hops. It's like dropping cream in your coffee.

"Milk stout had basically gone extinct in the United States. There were some oatmeal stouts around, but no milk stouts," Wallace said. "We did it once, and then we did it again. We put it into bombers; it was popular, made a couple of batches. And then a year later, we started putting it into six-packs, with the intent that it would be the winter seasonal. It just started going."

Milk Stout quickly became one of Left Hand's most popular beers. But when they started packaging it nitrogenized in 2011, it became their number-one seller—rare for a dark beer. Wallace called it "a disturbance in the force" because it subverted drinkers' expectations.

"People go, 'I didn't know beer could taste like this,'" Wallace said.

Brewpubs on Main

Wallace and Doore weren't the only ones who thought opening a brewery in the 1990s was a good idea. At a nearby aerospace company, Craig Taylor was trying to recruit Dennis Coombs to do the same.[24] Like most professional brewers, Taylor was a homebrewer tipsy on his tipple and saw a future in it. Coombs was game, as was Dave D'Epagnier, who overheard Taylor and Coombs talking shop. He, too, was a homebrewer and wanted in. Soon, Tom Charles was on board, and the foursome had momentum.

Now they needed a location.

Located on the northeast corner of Main Street and Sixth Avenue, Pumphouse Brewery took over the William Lugg Building, named after a prominent Longmont businessman from the early 1900s. The building had been host to various businesses—from wood and coal storage to a roller rink—but never a fire station. That didn't matter to Taylor and company; you need a theme to stand out, and a firehouse theme was as good as any.

But the William Lugg Building needed a lot of love. They worked days and spent nights chipping decades' worth of paint off the building's exposed bricks. Ross Hagen, who came with commercial brewpub experience, joined the team. In May 1996, Pumphouse Brewery & Restaurant opened with a firehouse décor and two similarly themed beers: Red Alert Amber and Wildflower Wheat.

It wasn't the only game in town. Located next door, the Overland Stage Stop Brewery was the first of the two to open its doors but didn't have the staying power. With a nine-barrel brewing system, Overland Stage Stop attracted Andrew Schwartz and Kent Waugh, two brewers working numerous positions at Rockies Brewing Company in Boulder.

Hailing from Ohio, Waugh was on his way to Montana for snowboarding when his car broke down in Fort Collins. Cooling his heels in a bar, Waugh was introduced to Fat Tire thanks to a few bar patrons. One sip sealed his fate, and Waugh decided to remain in Colorado and pursue brewing.

Featuring what Waugh called the "Colorado old-school line-up" (ESB, pale ale and stout), Overland didn't last long, but not because of the beer or location. As Waugh recalled, the owners argued, and then it closed. Both Wallace and Doore were silent partners at the Overland, but the person who took over the space and converted it to a taproom in the twilight of the decade would also take the craft beer revolution to new heights in the next: Dale Katechis.

7
THERE AND BACK AGAIN

Homebrewing in the Heart of Dixie wasn't commonplace in the 1980s. It wasn't commonplace in the 2000s, for that matter—the practice was illegal until 2013, despite homebrewing becoming federally legal in 1979.

That's one reason why Dale Katechis left, but it wasn't the only reason. Born and raised in Huntsville, Alabama, Katechis mostly grew up seventy-five miles west, in Florence, where he met his wife, Christi. The two attended Auburn University but had no designs of staying. Spurred by a 1991 *Outside* article listing Wise River, Montana, as one of the top ten places in the country to live—"Saw a picture of Wise River, Montana, and said, 'That's my life'"—the two packed up and headed west.

They ran out of money in Boulder. They stayed with Katechis's college roommate's sister, found odd jobs and fell in love with the Centennial State. Katechis started bartending at Old Chicago on Pearl Street before getting the opportunity to open the Longmont Old Chicago in 1996. The move brought Katechis closer to his home in Lyons (a small mountain town roughly twelve miles north by northwest of Longmont), but his tenure with the taphouse was soon to end.

"One day, at Old Chicago, a regional manager threw a calculator at my head, and I was like, 'Fuck this, I'm done. I'm going to go do it.'" *It* was a restaurant. Katechis grew up in the business, and it was his dream to open his own. All it took was one airborne calculator—and about $50,000 in advanced checks and credit cards.

"And we opened Oskar Blues April 25, on a Friday night, 1997, in a four-foot snowstorm," Katechis said with a grin. Named after two friends

Flagships

Every brewery has a number-one seller. Not every brewery has a flagship. When Dale's Pale Ale won the *New York Times* blind tasting, Oskar Blues had both.

Though the craft beer revolution's hallmarks were style, variety and choice, flagships legitimized the movement. It proved that craft brewers could brew excellence time and time again with the consistency of the big boys (Bud, Coors and Miller). Beers like Sierra Nevada Pale Ale, Samuel Adams Boston Lager and New Belgium Fat Tire traveled far and wide. They became spokesbeers for the breweries that birthed them and the revolution they sparked. They became synonymous with the movement and with quality. Take Fat Tire—practically every brewer interviewed in this book had a revelatory encounter with the amber ale (Katechis among them). It was a gateway to a world of flavors and a whole new career path.

Few could rival Fat Tire. Mountain Sun built a sisterhood of pubs and breweries on the back of Colorado Kind Ale, but it's hard to think of the laidback brewpubs and not picture a pint of pitch-black stout and the brewery's annual Stout Month tradition. Most associate Avery Brewing with its wide variety of big beers and experimentations, but not its bestseller White Rascal, accomplished though it is. Left Hand's Sawtooth Ale was number one until Milk Stout claimed the throne. Boulder Beer's Shake Chocolate Porter—first developed as an Old Chicago house brand—did the same at roughly the same time, unseating Hazed & Infused and Buffalo Gold.

Dale's Pale Ale was different. It became a national brand and a beer on which the brewery could hang its hat. Many Oskar Blues beers followed Dale, but none managed to overtake the "voluminously hopped mutha" of a pale. According to Katechis, some restaurants even mistook Dale as the name of the brewery, and at least one restaurant in New Jersey listed Mama's Little Yella Pils on its menu as Dale's Mama's Little Yella Pils.

Katechis met on a bike trip—Oskar and "Old Blue"—Oskar Blues Grill & Brews is an unlikely institution to set up in a town of 1,400.[25] The first year was quiet, and the house beer, Oskar, was brewed at Left Hand. One of Katechis's regulars, Craig Engelhorn, started badgering Katechis to brew his own.

"I set about teasing Dale that his new restaurant should have a brewery. After all, it was the 1990s, and we were in Colorado," Engelhorn told Virginia Miller in 2018.

A self-described "mediocre homebrewer," Katechis called Engelhorn's bluff. Engelhorn started looking and found a used six-barrel system built by legendary brewer Jim Schlueter in Santa Clarita, California, for sale. "We went out to see it, and it was in the guy's front yard, and his wife was standing in the front door," Katechis said. "It was a bitter divorce, and the brewpub was part of it."

The two brought the brewpub back to Lyons, stuck it in Oskar Blues' basement and contacted Brian Lutz, whom Katechis knew from the RedFish Brewery in Boulder. Katechis had a recipe dating to his college days at Auburn University. He and Engelhorn also had a shared affection for North Coast Brewing's Red Seal Ale. Add those to "Brian's commercial experience," and Dale's Pale Ale was born in July 1999.

"NOT JUST US CRAZY REDNECKS UP HERE."

Dale's Pale Ale was just the beginning, and Oskar Blues' success extended into the following decade with a series of milestones. In 2002, it began canning Dale's Pale Ale and expanded to a twenty-barrel system procured from Brian Dunn at Great Divide Brewing Company in Denver—the six-barrel Schlueter system moved out to the barn as an R&D brewery. In 2003, Frontier Airlines began carrying Dale's Pale Ale on its flights, and in 2005, the *New York Times* awarded Dale's Pale Ale "Best Pale Ale" in the country in a blind taste test.

"A can!" Eric Asimov wrote in the *New York Times* article. "Not long ago, cans represented all that was wrong with the assembly-line American beer industry. No craft brewer worth a copper brew kettle would even consider putting his precious ale in a can.[26] But times have changed, and some brewers say that cans are lighter and easier to recycle than bottles and offer complete protection against light."

Like every beer of the time, Dale's Pale Ale was first packaged in glass bottles. And like every other small brewery, it was done by hand and inefficiently. "Brian and I had this four-at-a-time filler," Katechis described. "You'd take twenty-two-ounce bottles, fill 'em; we'd hand-cap 'em, send 'em out.

"The goal was to hand-deliver them to local liquor stores and, hopefully, drive people to the front door of our restaurant," Katechis continued. "We knew the restaurant business more than we knew anything else. We're in a town of fourteen hundred people; we need to drive traffic to our front door."

Live music helped considerably, but nothing compared to the beer. Before Oskar Blues, Lyons was known as the gateway to the Rockies. Then came Dale's Pale Ale, and Lyons became the destination.

Next came a fax from Cask Brewing Systems in Calgary, Canada. It had developed a tabletop canning system that could package twelve-ounce beers, two at a time. It was well received in Canada—"Cans didn't have the stigma they do down here," Katechis said—but in America, it was a different story.

"We just laughed," Katechis said. So did attendees at the 2002 Craft Brewers Conference in Cleveland, Ohio, when Cask pitched the system. Some craft breweries across the nation had canned their beers: Wisconsin's Oshkosh Brewing Co. started canning its Chief Oshkosh Red Lager in 1991. Pete's Brewing, Capital Brewery, Brewski Brewing and James Page Brewing all had one-off cans, but they were packaged via contract at other facilities.

First introduced by Bill Coors in 1959, aluminum cans replaced tin cans—a problematic vessel for many reasons—as an inexpensive way to

Dale Katechis and Scott Waller using Oskar Blues' original cask tabletop canning system. *Courtesy Oskar Blues Brewery.*

ship beer long distances (aluminum weighs considerably less than glass). Aluminum also provided better protection for the beer, but in 2002, canned beer was the province of the big three: Bud, Miller and Coors. Craft beer was bottle-centric, partly because homebrewers could bottle and cap their beers at home, partly because glass bottles sent a signal to the consumer that their beer had more value than cheap, mass-market cans.

But Cask would not give up on Katechis.

"I give credit to Cask; they were extremely persistent," Katechis said. The company invited Katechis to see how the cans were made, and a few key points started to stand out: Cans were lightweight and easily recyclable, they could go where glass bottles could not and were easier to transport, both when it came to distribution and the customer's ability to take cans into the mountains.

"It kept hitting us," Katechis said. "It truly is a better vessel for beer." Katechis stopped laughing and then took out a Small Business Administrations loan and mortgaged the house. Three years later, Dale's Pale Ale won the *New York Times* blind tasting panel. "It was really that moment," Katechis said. "It's not just us crazy rednecks up here in Lyons."

The win validated Oskar Blues and pushed the brewery to the next level. "Years and years of triple-digit growth" followed. Katechis needed to expand.

HALF MILLION ON A NAPKIN

Katechis didn't want a second location; he just wanted to expand the first. But Oskar Blues Grill & Brews was one of many located in a nondescript Main Street strip mall, and Katechis was blocked from buying out the block. There were other issues: getting trucks in and out of downtown Lyons wasn't easy, and the small mountain town wasn't equipped for dealing with the amount of wastewater a brewery produces. Looking back, Katechis realized his inability to expand the Lyons brewpub was "a blessing in disguise," as was finding a space big enough in Longmont.

"We went from brewing in the basement in '99 to building a twenty-four-square-foot brewery and canning in a one-hundred-year-old barn in 2002," Katechis said. "[And then] moving into a thirty-five-thousand-square-foot building in Longmont because it was really all we could find."

Located in an industrial park across the street from a residential neighborhood, Oskar Blues Brewery and Tasty Weasel Taproom opened in 2008 with a little bit of luck from Katechis's bookkeeper.

"We got so lucky at every phase," Katechis said.

He needed it: Katechis had exhausted his funding and couldn't get any more, and he still needed a fifty-barrel brewhouse, or the whole venture would be sunk. Little did he know that his bookkeeper, an empty nester using Oskar Blues as a chance to get out of the house and do something, was independently wealthy.

"She was like, 'I'll loan you money,'" Katechis said. "It was a half-million-dollar loan, and she did it on a napkin."

In March 2008, Oskar Blues' Longmont brewery opened and produced 19,500 barrels of beer—an increase of 64 percent over the previous year (13,000 barrels), officially moving it from the Brewers Association's micro category to regional brewery status. And on December 12, 2012, Oskar Blues became the first brewery in Boulder County to open an East Coast base in Brevard, North Carolina.[27] The bathtub homebrewer from Alabama returned to the South with a state-of-the-art brewery in tow.

8
BEFORE THE GOLD RUSH, AFTER THE FLOOD

YOUR FRIENDLY NEIGHBORHOOD BREWERY

Despite impressive growth out of Left Hand and Oskar Blues, and consistent business from Pumphouse, the area's brewing scene was quiet throughout the 2000s. Then came the great recession, and things began to change. First to the table was the husband-and-wife duo Steve and Leslie Kaczeus.

"We wanted to be that neighborhood brewery," Leslie said. "I fell in love going to Bavaria and seeing people walk down the street with growlers in their hands. And they go to the local brewer and fill them up." Lucky for them, a small commercial space—1,200 square feet—was available not far from where they lived in Niwot. Even better, the landlord was an avid beer drinker.

Steve and Leslie hail from Boulder County—he from Boulder and she from Erie. The tech industry took them to California in 1989 and brought them back thirteen years later. But it was a homebrew kit Leslie gifted Steve for Christmas that changed everything.

"It was kind of an outlet for me to be creative," Steve said.

An ambitious homebrewer, Steve quickly graduated from extracts to all-grain brewing. And the beer was good. So good that they began wondering if a career in brewing was the viable next step. The tech industry was volatile, and a recent merger left Steve wondering if he would still have a job. He would, but the seed was planted and starting to sprout.

Charlie Papazian with Steve and Leslie Kaczeus. *Courtesy Bootstrap Brewing.*

They needed a test, so Steve attended a two-week seminar at the American Brewers Guild in 2011 "to learn how to brew from a technical perspective." Afterward, they would decide if they were going to open a brewery or try something else—maybe move to the Caribbean. But one look from Steve as he disembarked at the airport told Leslie the beach would have to wait.

"She just looked at me and said, 'I can tell,'" Steve said. "'We're starting a brewery, aren't we?'"

What followed should sound familiar at this point: The Kaczeuses visited area breweries, spoke with mentors, bought a used brewing system from Eddyline Brewery in Buena Vista, Colorado, and crafted an ambitious business plan—one they'd have to scale back considerably.

"We just couldn't raise any money," Leslie said.

"Nobody believed in us," Steve added. "We were kind of going through the [great recession]."

"They were like, 'You want to leave your high-tech jobs to do what?'" Leslie said.

With nowhere to turn, they hunkered down, made it small and put their life savings into it. And on June 20, 2012, the Kaczeuses opened Bootstrap

Bootstrap Brewing during the buildout. *Courtesy Bootstrap Brewing.*

Brewing Company—a nod to the brewery's DIY origins—with a three-and-a-half-barrel brewing system in about six hundred square feet of brewing space. It was cozy, to say the least.

"It resonated with us," Steve said. "All our friends and family came, and they helped us paint and build, put the chairs together. It really became a community brewery. It just blew up from there."

It also blew up because canning and distribution was part of the Kaczeuses' game plan from day one. Their first beer out the door was Insane Rush, an amber-hued IPA laced with potent hops and firm bitterness. "It became the best-selling IPA along the Front Range," Steve said.

Their second beer, Stick's Pale Ale, won gold at the 2016 GABF. Medals helped, but distribution helped more, and Bootstrap quickly grew, from 235 barrels in 2012 to just shy of 1,400 barrels in 2015.

"Peaceful, Communal Feeling."

Bootstrap Brewing was one of seven breweries to open in Boulder County in 2012. It was "Wild West type openings," Jeffrey Green said. "[People were] taking the resources they had without going through giant investment firms and having a lot of investors."

Twenty-six miles southwest of Bootstrap, in a town a quarter the size of Niwot, Jeffrey and Susan Green opened their humbly named Very Nice Brewing Company in the mountain town of Nederland.

Breweries were opening left and right across the county and across the country. And the playing field was still level. At the Great American Beer Festival that October, "Russian River's booth looked exactly like Very Nice's booth. Avery's booth looked exactly like Very Nice," Green said. It was still egalitarian and "felt like we're just brewers."

Born in Dayton, Ohio, Green first came to the Centennial State as a kid on vacation. "It seemed like adventure was around every corner," he said. "It was just heaven." The trip planted the seed in Green's mind, and in 1999, he moved to the area, settling first in Denver before relocating to Boulder, moving incrementally closer and closer to the mountains until he was in them.

Brewing came at the turn of the century when he hooked up with former Wolf Tongue brewer Cory O'Neel. Their first beer was a clone of McEwan's Export, a mass-manufactured Scottish ale.[28] "I had recently gone on a backpacking tour, and I fell in love with that beer," Green said.

Green fell in love with more than just beer across the pond. "I fell in love with the English pub," he said. "After your day, you go to the pub, and you're talking to everyone from eighteen to eighty that sits there and talks about their day."

Luckily for Green, Boulder had a version of the welcoming and communal English pub: Mountain Sun. "I remember going to see Yonder

Above: Jeffrey Green building out Very Nice Brewing Company. *Courtesy Very Nice Brewing Company.*

Opposite: Jeffrey and Susan Green. *Courtesy Very Nice Brewing Company.*

Mountain String Band in the Mountain Sun," Green said. "You knew they were going to be there every Sunday, and you saw the same people every week, and the beer was excellent. I would say my first true craft beer love was the Java Porter.

"You were wrapping up your weekend, you had to go to work the next day, but at least you had that last little awesome thing before you had to start your week again," Green continued. "And that feeling was a very peaceful, communal feeling—it wasn't like a party feeling that you go to a bar and people are doing shots off skis and TVs everywhere.…The craft beer space was definitely closer to the pub space."

That's what Green wanted to offer. Very Nice would be a place where locals could come to drink, talk and listen to live music. "It worked for us," Green said. "When we hit the market, it was something Nederland needed at the time."

When Very Nice opened in October 2012, it was the first brewery in Nederland to serve only beer.[29] And since Very Nice opened during the 2012 brewery craze, Green could get his brewer's feet under him.

"At the time, there was a lot of grace amongst craft beer drinkers and the craft beer world, where you could start off with rough edges—your beer having rough edges and not being perfect," Green explained. "You would almost get an excitement, where people would like this, or not like this. They would talk about it; there would be conversations. And it was just a lot of fun, having that process.

"Back then, you had this sense of just being able to bootstrap it, being able to take the resources you have without going leagues into debt and carving yourself out a little niche in the beer world," he continued.

In 2012, that niche was still growing. Eschewing distribution, Green opened Very Nice on a 3.5-barrel system and sold beer over the counter. In 2013, Very Nice brewed and sold 119 barrels of beer. They doubled the following year and cracked 275 barrels in 2015—less than 1 percent of Avery Brewing's output in Boulder.

"It really isn't solely about the beer," Green said. "It's about the space that we create. We're always going to be the guys who're going to sponsor the little league team, keep people happy with being able to come in and feel safe, friendly, good place to hang out and talk about your day," he continued. "There will always be the small little guy like my wife and I, who are going to be there no matter what."

After the Flood

In 1992, Longmont, Lyons, Nederland and Niwot were home to zero breweries.

"We started the first one, and we helped our friends start the second one," Eric Wallace of Left Hand Brewing Company said. "Now, there's a bunch."

"Brewed on the banks of the mighty St. Vrain," read the labels on Left Hand beer bottles. As *Colorado Breweries* author Dan Rabin pointed out, the reference to *mighty* was tongue-in-cheek, as the St. Vrain Creek lazily winds its way around Lyons, skirts Hygiene and cuts right through Longmont.

But from September 11 to 15, 2013, Longmont experienced the most devastating flash flood in its history. While once-in-a-lifetime natural disasters have ways of destroying budding industries, the areas surrounding the St. Vrain bounced back stronger than before. A new wave of industry was coming, and nothing signaled this more than closing the Butterball turkey processing plant in 2011.

When the Butterball plant was built in 1950, Longmont's primary industry was agriculture. Sixty-one years later, Butterball was the last vestige of those days, wiped out by booms in retail, as well as housing and residential amenities.

The first start-up brewery to open in Longmont since the Pumphouse in 1996, 300 Suns Brewing, planned to open in late 2013 but had to wait because of flooding during construction. Many businesses suffered a similar fate or worse.

On February 21, 2014, 300 Suns Brewing—owned and operated by husband and wife Dan and Jean Ditslear—was the first brewery to open in Butterball's shadow. Like most craft breweries at the time, the location was removed from the city's walkable portions, but the focus was hyperlocal, reliant on good beer and cultivated a following of curious drinkers.

Less than a mile away, Shoes & Brews was another family establishment started by Ashlee and Colin Anderson; their friend from college, Dave Zakavec; Colin's father, Roger; and Ashlee's friends, Kris and Mike Donohoe. The sextet opened the doors on July 1, 2014, along the banks of the St. Vrain in one of the many flooded buildings.

When they moved in, the space was one big room with two bathrooms in the back. They built a wall bisecting the room and put a retail running store in the front and a bar with a one-barrel brewing system in the back.

"Everything you see, we built," Ashlee Anderson said.

The original model was based on something similar to a brewpub—"shoes will pay for brews," Anderson said—but when they opened, they realized that the businesses complemented each other.

"It's its own wonderful thing," Anderson said. "If you had to separate the businesses, you could. But the fun thing is, you don't have to."

Now married, Ashlee and Colin weren't when they started their Shoes & Brews journey. Neither were Ryan and Robin Wibby when they opened the doors to Wibby Brewing in September 2015. That changed at the 2017 GABF when Wibby Brewing won silver for its Moondoor Dunkel. While accepting the award on stage, Ryan dropped to one knee and popped the question.

The win and proposal generated headlines, but Wibby's eclectic lagers kept the doors open and the tanks full.

Born in Golden, Colorado, Wibby picked up a love for lager in Pennsylvania while working at Iron Hill Brewery in Lancaster. He turned passion into profession with a six-month certified brewmaster course at Berlin, Germany's VLB.[30] There, he settled on a combination: traditional German lagers melded with American ingenuity. "Technically, it's more difficult to make a crisp, clean lager that's good to drink," Wibby said. "Our goal is anything an ale can make, a lager can make better."

Ryan Wibby proposes, and Robin accepts at the 2017 Great American Beer Festival. *Courtesy Brewers Association.*

Shoes & Brews—shoes in the front, brews in the back. *Author photo.*

Like 300 Suns, Wibby Brewing opened near the shuttered Butterball plant, this time on the north side of the facility at 209 Emery Street. At the time, both breweries operated in industrial-like settings. But in April 2015, construction crews began tearing down the shuttered concrete plant. The area would be reenvisioned and revitalized as the South Main Station apartment complex. Across Main Street, Anderson pointed out a whole activity complex cropping up around Shoes & Brews. "This area has really become a center for people who are looking to be more active," Anderson said.

Powder Keg Brewing Company became the second brewery in Niwot—located less than a half-mile from Bootstrap—in July 2014. Großen Bart Brewery (pronounced "grossen"; the name is German for "big beard") wasn't far behind, opening in November 2014 with a ten-barrel system in a spacious facility a half-mile from Shoes & Brews. And two miles west of Großen Bart, Skyeye Brewing opened in June 2015.

In Boulder County, the brewing world wasn't just expanding; it was accelerating.

PART III

AND BEYOND

9

"THAT'S A GREAT IDEA, CHARLIE."

As the saying goes, all roads lead to Rome. By the time the craft beer revolution rolled around, those roads led to Charles Papazian. The progenitor of the American Homebrewers Association and the Brewers Association, the architect behind the Great American Beer Festival and the World Beer Cup, the driving force behind periodicals *Zymurgy* and the *New Brewer* and the author of the best-selling homebrewing book *The Complete Joy of Homebrewing* was born on January 23, 1949, in Glen Ridge and raised twenty miles south in Warren Township, New Jersey. College took him to Charlottesville, Virginia, and a man homebrewing with Blue Ribbon malt took him over the edge.

In 1967, Papazian enrolled in the University of Virginia's navy ROTC program but realized three years later that it wasn't the place for him. Though he would leave five years later with a bachelor's degree in nuclear engineering, Papazian dabbled. He took classes in art, medicine and education.

"I was probably an average to better-than-average student, but I wasn't an A student," Papazian told Theresa McCulla in 2017. "I just liked the experiences of discovering new stuff."

Papazian also enjoyed going out and having a few beers with friends—not for the taste of the beer but for the social aspect of drinking with friends. The taste—that was atrocious. You could snag a six-pack for sixty-nine cents, and it was insipid stuff. There had to be another way.

Charlie Papazian. *Courtesy Charlie Papazian.*

That's when George Conner entered Papazian's life. Conner was a beer drinker and a *Finnegans Wake* aficionado. He taught Papazian the Japanese game of Go and told Papazian that he had a neighbor who made his own beer, "Prohibition-style homebrew, classic."

Beer made in the home?

Yep, wanna try some?

The year was 1970, and Papazian tried his first homebrew. The beer they had was a year old, "somewhat cidery, but not overly so," and had something those sixty-nine-cent six-packs didn't: flavor.

The homebrew that turned Papazian on probably wasn't too much more refined than the average beer at the time, but it "had more character to it, more personality than the very watered down, fizzy yellow beer that we were drinking as college students."

Plus, a person made this beer—not a faceless and generic company. This beer had a story, a tale transmitted in every sip. Papazian was hooked.

Conner and Papazian got the recipe, eight lines written down on a three-by-five notecard: hop-flavored Blue Malt extract, sugar, yeast and water. They started brewing. The first couple of batches were awful. They used bread yeast and not beer yeast; they used cane sugar and not brewing sugar. The malt and hop extracts they used came from the supermarket.

But they learned and experimented, and the more they brewed, the better the beer got. When Papazian relocated to Boulder in 1972, he found homebrew and winemaking stores offering grains, hops and different malt extracts: stouts, ales and lagers.[31] Back in Charlottesville (and practically everywhere else), all the beer bought off the shelf looked the same and tasted the same. But for a homebrewer, a world of flavors, aromas and styles awaited.

In 1972, homebrew was still a hobby for Papazian. He landed in Boulder in the middle of a recession and needed work. After a brief stint on a shoe assembly line and as a janitor at a shopping mall, the homebrewer with a degree in nuclear engineering landed a gig teaching preschool.

For eight years, Papazian was a grade school teacher by day and homebrew teacher by night. He estimated one thousand or so students passed through his homebrew class, and some of his early students went pro—Jeff Lebesch (New Belgium Brewery) and Russell Scherer (Wynkoop Brewing Company) to name two. His classes became more popular, and Papazian refined his approaches and tweaked his techniques. A three- to four-page syllabus for the class expanded to nine. It was the beginning of a book, *The Joy of Brewing*, a seventy-eight-page self-published manifesto pounded out on a borrowed IBM Selectric typewriter in 1976.[32]

An early copy of *The Joy of Homebrewing. Courtesy Brewers Association.*

ZYMURGY T.M.

Journal of the American Homebrewers Association [T.M.]

Volume 1 Number 1 Copyright 1978, *Zymurgy* December 1978

The Lost Art of Homebrewing

—*by Karl F. Zeisler*

While rummaging through the basement the other day I came unexpectedly upon a curious and at first unrecognizable bit of mechanism; on examination it proved to be a device I once had purchased hopefully for filtering homebrew. The discovery took me right back to pre-New Deal times, the days before the respectable art of homebrewing faded into a poignant past along with candle-molding, lard-rendering, and curry-combing. Memories returned of agonizing experiments with patent filters, cappers, siphons, bottle washers, and yeast—all those devices which characterized my humble beginning as a homebrewer—and I recalled vividly the last batch I ever concocted, the one I spent an hour wiping off the kitchen ceiling. That catastrophe, on an evening when my wife was entertaining, cured me even without her final ultimatum. Foolishly, I had allowed several bottles to warm up: the second one let go as I pried off the cap and sprayed the whole kitchen, including the supper over which my wife had lovingly labored. I had made the usual mistake of putting my thumb over the bottle, and so the suds lathered my bosom. After the bottle had finished fizzing, the room looked like the scene of a hatchet murder, and there was a good half inch of beer on the floor.

This explosion terminated years of painful, groping experiments, as far as I was concerned, experiments that had often resulted in disaster, occasionally in a fluid that was actually drinkable, and once or twice, as in any hazardous pursuit, in a marvellously delectable, amber-clear, ivory-collared treasure, to be fondled, held up to the light, and sipped delicately—a gift from the gods as rare as truth from a barrister's lips, and as palatable as manna. It had been

continued on page 8

Congress Passes Homebrew

It's official. If you're eighteen years or older, you may legally brew one hundred gallons of beer for personal use each year—tax free! This probably isn't an astonishing piece of news, as beer-making has been legal in the minds of homebrewers for years.

On October 14, 1978, President Carter signed a bill, H.R. 1337, which dealt primarily with excise taxes on

continued on page 12

Zymurgy issue number one. *Courtesy Brewers Association.*

Papazian was transitioning from teacher to writer. In October 1978, President Jimmy Carter signed H.R. 1337 and legalized homebrewing on a federal level. Two months later, Papazian and friend Charlie Matzen published the first issue of *Zymurgy*—twelve hand-fashioned pages of recipes, musings, reporting, cartoons, advertisements and the announcement of the first annual National Homebrew Competition set to take place in Boulder, Colorado, sometime in May 1978.

Homebrew was here to stay.

The faithful were flocking to Boulder; within a year, homebrewing went commercial at Boulder Brewing. Then came Beer & Steer, a two-day potluck party for four hundred, complete with live music and plenty of homebrew, at Heil Valley Ranch, up Left Hand Canyon northwest of Boulder.

"It was remote; we had our own electric system, we had our own port-a-potty," Papazian said. "We had our own everything."

H.R. 1337—Ninety-Fifth Congress (1977–78)

Introduced to the House of Representatives on January 4, 1977, H.R. 1337 sought to correct a law left on the books following the repeal of Prohibition in 1933. Though the Twenty-First Amendment overrode the Eighteenth, legalizing the sale, distribution and consumption of alcohol in the United States, it did not repeal the excise tax on homebrewing. This was most likely due to oversight, but it remained on the books until 1978.

"The federal Bureau of Alcohol, Tobacco and Firearms essentially adopted a hear-no-evil, see-no-evil approach to enforcement, and there is no record of any American, including those who ran homebrewing shops, being arrested for homebrewing when it was illegal," Tom Acitelli wrote in *The Audacity of Hops*.

U.S. senator Alan Cranston (D-California) called the law "dopey." It was, by and large, inert. As Papazian recounted years later, one of the students in his homebrewing class was an ATF agent and, dressed like an ATF agent, stuck out like a sore thumb. Papazian skirted any issues by reminding the class that homebrewing was illegal and not to sell it.

Whether the agent was there to take names or learn how to homebrew has been lost to the ether—nothing came of the event, which slightly bummed Papazian out. "Think of the publicity," he would say with a laugh.

Enforced or not, a law is a law. And when Representative William A. Steiger (R-Wisconsin) introduced H.R. 1337, Senator Cranston sponsored the bill with an amendment that would strike the excise tax of the hobby on a federal level: "Allows any adult (formerly only heads of families) to produce wine and beer for personal and family use and not for sale without incurring the wine or beer excise taxes or any penalties for quantities per calendar year of: (1) 200 gallons if there are two or more adults in the household and (2) 100 gallons if there is only one adult in the household."

The measure was presented to President Jimmy Carter on October 4, 1978, who signed it on October 14. On February 1, 1979, homebrewing was once again legal on a federal level.

They were also good stewards of the land. They picked up after themselves and left only trampled grass. The owners welcomed them back, and the word got out. Friends of friends of friends started showing up at homebrew classes. More came to Beer & Steer.

"That was an interesting time, not only for beer but culturally," Papazian said, "[of] people opening their minds to consider new ideas. The way they do things and the way they consume things."

And the way they share things. Drinking homebrew wasn't just about you try my beer, and I'll try yours; it was also a process of sharing observations and tricks. Papazian's classes were group learning. Beer & Steer was group sharing. *Zymurgy* was both and more. A born leader since his days organizing clubhouse activities back in New Jersey, Papazian was at the center of them all.[33]

"When you're drinking good beer, enjoying homebrew, you come up with ideas," Papazian said. "Oftentimes, those ideas get out of hand and get some legs."

A professional brewing scene was building. And in 1981, Papazian, Stuart Harris, Frank Morris and Tom Burns started noodling out the idea that would become the GABF, "where we could celebrate what was left of American beer."

Charlie Papazian makes an entrance at the 1985 Homebrewers Convention. *Courtesy Brewers Association.*

Harris was a software engineer writing *Zymurgy* articles on the side. Morris worked at Liquor Mart, which held Boulder's first retail liquor license after the city went wet in 1968, but it was Burns, the second brewmaster of Boulder Brewing, who connected the foursome with the Brewers Association of America (BAA). The BAA represented the remaining regional breweries, and it was curious if these microbreweries were going to do anything.

"[Tom Burns] presented himself in a way as a maverick and as a new age brewer," Papazian said, adding that the old brewing guard making up the regional breweries liked him. "Because of Tom and his relationship with these people, they kind of trusted what he was up to."

With a little backing, Papazian and his circle began researching who could come to a festival and what they would serve. *Beers of America*, a book of beer labels—"page after page of beer labels"—became the guide.

"We looked through that book and were able to determine what Yuengling was brewing. What August Schell was brewing," Papazian said. "We saw that bock was being made. Oktoberfest was being made. Porters and stouts were being made....Sierra Nevada was operational; Boulder Beer was operational; Anchor Brewing was operational."[34]

They figured out what to serve, and now they needed to get it to Colorado. Eddie Miller, one of Papazian's students, was a beer importer, and he owned a trucking company. Miller handled logistics. Papazian locked down a ballroom at Boulder's Harvest House Hotel but ran into complications when the ownership changed hands three months after inking the deal.

A beer festival? The new owners were skeptical. "'What the hell is this all about?'" Papazian recounts. "'We're not doing this.'"

Well, you have a contract, Papazian pleaded with the suits. It was an interrogation scene straight out of a noir movie, and Papazian held his own. In the end, the hotel owners relented, even if they were worried about the carpet. "This idea was so out of bounds," Papazian said with a smile.

Attendants of the first GABF, all eight hundred of them, enjoyed eight-ounce samples of forty-seven beers from twenty-four breweries.

They learned a lot. For starters, eight-ounce samples were "a little too much enjoyment." The second festival was held outside the Harvest House, under a big tent. This time, a trampled lawn wore out their welcome, and GABF got the boot. The festival relocated to the Curigan Exhibition Hall in Denver in 1984—"that was a leap of faith that went splat"—bounced to the Regency Hotel from 1985 to 1987, spent 1988 and 1989 at the Denver Merchandise Mart and then went back to Currigan Hall until 2004, when the festival relocated permanently to the redesigned Colorado Convention Center.

The 1993 Great American Beer Festival at Currigan Exhibition Hall in Denver. *Courtesy Brewers Association.*

"Like any business, it was growing pains," Papazian recalled. "We grew and grew a lot—never made money." The cash flow was good; they just kept breaking even. "It was hard to figure out, financially, how to make it work without spending as much as you were bringing in," Papazian said.

In 2001, Nancy Johnson took over duties as festival director. "She's a wizard," Papazian said, particularly her ability to keep the festival relevant while beer festivals cropped up left and right throughout the decades. "I'm sure people imagine that being first is romantic and terrific and so fun and adventurous," Papazian said. "Well, yeah, maybe that's part of it, but it's hairy as well."

Papazian's GABF horror stories range from snowfall on opening night to tornadoes threatening tents to transportation accidents. "There was one story [from 1982], where the truck driver went through a tunnel in Pennsylvania, and he didn't pay attention to the clearance," Papazian recalled. "Ripped the top—half the top—off this semi. The oncoming car had rocks and damage, but no one was hurt."

Driving the oncoming car involved in the accident was one of the daughters of the Yuenglings. Coincidences abound when Papazian is around.

Styles and Variety Were the Goal

"For the first time in decades, the American beer consumer is beginning to see the possibility of choice," exclaimed the 1982 summer issue of *Zymurgy*, announcing the first GABF. Neither the words *micro* nor *craft* appeared in the seven paragraphs outlining the festival. Choice was front and center, as was the declaration, "Every attempt has been made to conscientiously represent the most unique, special and quality beers brewed in the U.S."

In 1983, GABF introduced the consumer preference poll, which allowed guests to vote for their favorite beers. That year, Sierra Nevada took home first and second place, respectively, for Pale Ale and Porter. Anchor nabbed third with its Anchor Porter.

In 1985, then six-week-old Boston Beer Company missed the truck, and founder Jim Koch air freighted twenty cases of Samuel Adams Boston Lager just in time to make the festival. That year, Boston Lager took the top prize in the consumer preference poll.

It wouldn't be the only year Samuel Adams won the poll, an award that would court a fair amount of controversy and consternation—both in how Koch attracted votes and how he marketed his victories. In 1987, Papazian and festival cofounder Daniel Bradford instituted a professional blind tasting

Great American Beer Festival founders Charlie Papazian and Daniel Bradford. *Courtesy Brewers Association.*

of beers categorized by style, twelve in all, with gold, silver and bronze medals awarded.[35] But Samuel Adams still walked away with the consumer preference poll, this time for its Festival Lager.

Though the consumer preference poll proved to be more a source of derision than acclaim—it was discontinued in 1990—the official competition based on beer styles that arose from it might be GABF's greatest legacy. Its objectivity lent legitimacy to the beers awarded, and its celebration of historical and regional styles instilled a level of creativity in brewers heretofore unseen. From the original twelve, GABF's competition blossomed to ninety-two competitive categories in 2015, with over 6,600 beers competing for gold, silver and bronze medals that year.

"Some styles of beer were close to extinction before the new brewing revival in America saved them from the archival tombs," Papazian wrote in *Microbrewed Adventures*. "We have created the American Beer Ark to float above the light-lagered oceans of the world, harboring with care and passionate enthusiasm the great beer traditions of the world."

BEER EQUALS COMMUNITY

In 1983, Papazian spun the Institute for Fermentation & Brewing Studies—also known as the Institute for Brewing Studies before morphing into the Association of Brewers (AOB)—from the American Homebrewers Association to work with the commercial sector. In 2005, the AOB and the BAA merged to create one trade group representing America's small and independent brewers: the Brewers Association (BA).

Headquartered in Boulder, the BA appointed Papazian president and brought all of his various creations—the American Homebrewers Association, the Great American Beer Festival, the World Beer Cup, *Zymurgy* and the *New Brewer* and Brewers Publications—under one roof. If the craft beer world had a nucleus, Boulder was it.

And the connective tissue holding it all together: community. Asked to reflect on the legacy of homebrew, Papazian commonly recounted a watershed observation from his early days of drinking sixty-nine-cent six-packs: The beer was stupid, and it made those who drank it stupid to boot. Homebrew was different. When people got together to drink homebrew, they talked about homebrew. They recounted stories of its creation and the history of its tradition. Homebrew created a community.

Beer writer Michael Jackson at the 1983 Great American Beer Festival. *Courtesy Brewers Association.*

It also attracted one. "Well over 90 percent of the craft breweries in America were started by homebrewers," Papazian wrote in the introduction to the fourth edition of *The Complete Joy of Homebrewing*.

During the January 2012 Brewers Association dinner with the board of directors and the BA's staff, then directors chair Sam Calagione recounted the creation of the Pro-Am Competition at the GABF. Introduced in 2006, GABF's Pro-Am paired amateurs with professionals to make a beer for the competition. Rare is the industry where the two are allowed to collaborate, but, as Calagione pointed out, "so many of us moved between those lines to make that community grow."

Jackson, again from *The Complete Joy of Homebrewing*'s preface, concurred: "I have occasionally commented that many homebrewers in the United States are more knowledgeable than some of the professionals. The analogy I would make is with sports-car buffs and line managers in Detroit. The hobbyist has encountered every kind of engine or gearbox, and knows how to improvise and be creative. The line manager may in some instances know only the model to which his plant is dedicated."

As Calagione continued in his 2012 speech, citing a Sam Shepard play, *Fool for Love*, "It's the same love. Just got split in two, that's all."

10

A HOBBY GONE BERSERK

By the turn of the twenty-first century, the story of beer in Boulder County became a variation on a theme—homebrewer parlays passion into profession. Some were retired and looking for something new. Others were just joining the workforce and refused to join the nine-to-fivers. Some came from the tech industry and others from hospitality. Regardless, what was once a cottage industry became standardized. Going to a bank to secure a loan to start a brewery was no longer unheard of. Manufacturers made equipment for breweries of all sizes. Raw materials were easy to come by. Periodicals like *All About Beer* (first published in 1979 and acquired by Daniel Bradford in 1992) to the *New Brewer* (established in 1984 by Charlie Papazian's Institute for Fermentation and Brewing Studies) to Fort Collins–based *Craft Beer & Brewing* (founded in 2013 as part of the Unfiltered Media Group, LLC) provided a wealth of information. Toss the multitude of technical books published by Brewers Publication into the mix, and the tricks of the trade were on the table. Hands-on experience could easily be acquired, from classes to certifications, and it wasn't hard to attract professional brewers to jump ship at their current place to join yours.

The scene was exploding, and in Boulder County, thirteen breweries and brewpubs were operating at the dawn of 2010. By the end of 2015, nearly thirty more would join their ranks.

Tom Horst was the first, and the smallest, to the foray. Hailing from Hudson, South Dakota, Horst followed his sister to the Centennial State in the 1980s, set up shop teaching instrumental music at Boulder High School

Promo photo of Charlie Papazian for the 1984 Microbrewery Conference. *Courtesy Brewers Association.*

and stayed there for twenty-eight years. As he was getting ready to retire, his wife, Kristy, asked what he planned to do next.

Why don't you start a brewery? Kristy offered.

Why not, indeed? Horst had been homebrewing since the early 1990s—the first recipe he and his son brewed was Papazian's Rocky Raccoon honey lager from *The Complete Joy of Homebrewing*—and going pro seemed like a good way to keep busy. And Boulder County had a home occupation law, which meant Horst could commercially brew out of their two-car detached garage.

On May 10, 2010, the Horsts opened the Crystal Springs Brewing Company out of their home in Sunshine Canyon.

Brewing on a twenty-gallon system, two-thirds of a barrel, an official told Horst that he had the smallest brewery in the country and was the first to start in the garage. It was quaint and cozy, and exactly what they wanted. They sold to four liquor stores and two restaurants, all within a one-mile radius of their place. But it was the restaurants, specifically the second, Pizzeria Locale, that put them over. Coke goes better with this pizza than wine, the owner told Horst, how about selling us your Summertime Kölsch?[36]

Both Pizzeria Locale and Horst underestimated how popular the beer would be. Horst; graduated to a two-barrel system in the garage to keep up with demand, but by 2012, they needed to expand to a larger facility.

LOUISVILLE

Located ten miles southeast of Boulder, Louisville transitioned from a mining town to a suburb in the 1950s. Its first brewery, the Majestic Brewing Company, set up shop at the twilight of the twentieth century, at 270 South Taylor Avenue. It aimed to create the perfect beer for women, which resulted in a nine-month research project that led public relations director June Davidson to cream ale.

"Golden in color, creamy in consistency, yet light on the palate and of course, sympathetic to the waistline," Davidson told the *New Brewer* in 2000. "Hence, the brewing of Anu, a cream ale. In Celtic mythology, Anu is the ancestral and universal mother of the Celts.

"For too long, women have had to go along with what has been primarily a beer developed for the male palate," Davidson continued. "No other brewery has addressed the issue that more and more women are interested in drinking beer. So, why not have one which can sit alongside what's already offered but addresses what women want—an alternative to wine and hard liquor."

The concept didn't last. According to the following year's *New Brewer*, Majestic Brewing had closed and moved production to Europe. The business was administratively dissolved with the Colorado secretary of state on May 1, 2002.

In the mid- to late 2000s, Rock Bottom Restaurant & Brewery set up a large production facility in Louisville.[37] It wasn't until Gravity Brewing opened in late summer 2012 that Louisville reentered Boulder County's craft brewing scene.

Located at 1150 Pine Street, Gravity Brewing is housed in a building owned by the American Legion (Walter Rhoades Post 111). The Legion had more space than it knew what to do with and needed a way of bringing in some income. Its answer: convert the ballroom area and rent it out.

Wild Goose Canning

A quarter-mile east of Crystal Springs, as the crow flies, Wild Goose Canning resides, a key player in the craft beer canning revolution.

Founded in 2009 as Wild Goose Engineering in Boulder, Wild Goose joined the brewing industry because of sheer location. Its next-door neighbor, Upslope Brewing Company, was expanded on the success of its pale ale and India pale ale. And it was canning all of its beers using the standard Cask Brewing Systems hand canner, which did five cans per minute. To empty one thirty-barrel bright tank of beer resulted in two shifts a day, six days a week of labor. There had to be a faster way, owner Matt Cutter and brewer Dany Page figured. Maybe the engineering company next door could help?

"So, Dany and Alexis Foreman and Jeff [Aldred, cofounders of Wild Goose] went down this long, painful path of developing a canning line that they had cobbled together with a rafting frame, our seamer from Cask and this filler from Niagara Dispensing [Technologies] that was intended to fill cups of beer in stadiums in three seconds," Upslope's Matt Cutter said.

They hooked it all together with a conveyor connecting each station, and eureka! "We got that thing up to seventeen cans per minute," Cutter said. "And then, eventually, twenty-four cans per minute and then twenty-six cans a minute.

"Wild Goose Engineering stopped doing everything else they were doing as part of that company. They got into the canning line business."

Their timing was perfect. The brewing industry was taking off like a rocket, and those who were packaging were reaching for cans. In an interview with *Company Week*, Wild Goose cofounder Aldred said the company took in about $10 million in 2015 and predicted it would surpass $15 million in 2016—with customers as far-flung as Australia. In 2016, the company merged with Meheen Manufacturing (a bottling line out of Washington), and in 2018, Wild Goose Canning moved its headquarters to Louisville.

Around about 2010, longtime homebrewer John Frazee and friend Ryan Bowers decided to partner to open a brewery. They attracted Julius Hummer—son of Boulder Beer's cofounder David Hummer—to head up brewing operations and spent a year raising funds and the next looking for a place to call home. When they came across the Legion's offer, the trio took over the building's west side and started brewing up high-gravity beers.[38] One of their initial beers, Acceleration Double IPA, weighed in at 9.8 percent alcohol by volume and ninety-eight international bittering units (9.8 meters per second squared is the rate of acceleration).

Hummer didn't stay long at Gravity, but the IPA did. Meanwhile, a few blocks east, on Louisville's main drag, Jon Howland opened 12Degree Brewing in the summer of 2013 with Belgian-style beers and Belgian-influenced eats.[39] That October, Crystal Springs found some space in an office park southeast of town, relocated the two-barrel brewhouse and brewed twenty-four hours a day. In the spring of 2014, it expanded to a fifteen-barrel system with thirty-barrel fermenters and brewed nearly three hundred barrels of beer.

"It's been quite the ride from that little two-thirds-barrel system," Horst said in 2019.

ERIE

East of Louisville, Erie was one of Colorado's coal towns, settled in 1867 and incorporated seven years later. It was also a wet town, which meant saloons. There were no breweries, though. Those wouldn't come until October 2013, when the father-son duo of Tim Suttman and Nate Cervantes opened the Industrial Revolution Brewing Company smack-dab in the middle of a neighborhood.

Like many before them, Suttman was a homebrewer, and Cervantes picked up a taste for German culture while abroad. The two decided to give Erie what the city was missing.

Ditto for Echo Brewing. Its journey began in the nearby town of Frederick in 2012 when the Richards family—Erie residents Melissa; twin brothers, Daniel and Dennis; and sister Katy Dukes and her husband, Shannon—opened a seven-barrel brewing operation. Two years later, they decided to open a second location closer to home and converted a firehouse on Briggs Street into 2,500 square feet of pizzeria and brewpub. They opened Echo Brewing Cask and Barrel in September 2014. Twelve months before, anyone in Erie wanting to drink at the source had to leave town. Now they had two taprooms from which to choose.

We Have Laws for These Kinds of Things

In many respects, Colorado still has roots in the Wild West. Often, you'll find people and businesses doing what they want without necessarily abiding by the law—or even knowing what the law is.

Take, for instance, Charlie Papazian's homebrew classes, which weren't technically legal at the time. Jump ahead about two decades, and Eric Wallace and Dick Doore were trying to figure out how to make some money with Left Hand Brewing Company. They were brewing and bottling, and people were coming up to the brewery to see what was going on. These curious drinkers were given a tour and sent on their way with a growler to two—but not without a few free samples.

"They're like, 'You should charge me,'" Wallace told Theresa McCulla in 2017. "And I was like, 'I don't know if I can.'"

As Wallace recalled, Colorado Brewing Company, located in Thornton, had a salesroom and a tasting room, "selling beers over there like they were some kind of pub," he recounted. "So we call up Laura Harris [at the Liquor Enforcement Division] and said, 'Hey, we hear that these guys'—we didn't want to get them in trouble—'we hear these guys are, you know, are legally able to sell beer by the pint.'

"We asked her how, and she said, 'Well, yeah. Here is how it works. And this is what you may and may not do.' So, she kind of laid the road map out for us of how to do it."

So, Wallace and Doore put their taproom together, and the news got around. Odell Brewing called and so did Bristol Brewing in Colorado Springs. "And then everyone started calling each other," Wallace continued. "We were all trying to figure it out."

Lafayette

Founded in 1888 by coal mine owner Mary Miller (the town is named after her late husband), Lafayette was home to no breweries pre- and post-Prohibition. Miller was a teetotaler and prohibited the sale of spirituous, vinous and malt liquors east of what is now Public Road.

But she didn't say anything about the west side of the street. Though the saloons won the battle, Miller's side won the war in 1916, when Colorado became one of the first states to go dry. Four years later, Prohibition was a federal decree.

Nearly a century later, Lafayette got its first craft brewery. Two families—Barb, Ron and Austin Hoglund and Torianna and Mitchell Nichols—came together to open the Front Range Brewing Company in a strip mall west of Public Road (Mary would be proud) in July 2013.

One month later, Chicagoans Kristin and Ryan Scott opened the doors to Odd13 Brewing on Simpson Street, east of South Public Road. (Sorry, Mary.)

The Scotts started cranking out West Coast–style IPAs on a 10-barrel system, and the business grew—from 150 barrels in 2013 to almost 700 in 2014. In 2015, Odd13 picked up a second location, a production brewery with a 30-barrel brewhouse, and tapped New England transplant Eric Larkin as the head brewer. Larkin wanted to try his hand at making New England–style IPAs (also known as hazy/juicy IPAs), popularized by Vermont's the Alchemist.[40] Odd13's taproom brewer, Brandon Boldt, who also hailed from the East Coast, was eager to experiment, but Ryan Scott wasn't.

"I put a ton of effort into producing finished beers that didn't look like homebrew," Scott told *Beer Advocate* in 2017.

Kristin and Ryan Scott of Odd13 Brewing atop Mount Sanitas. *Courtesy of Odd13 Brewing.*

Larkin and Boldt persisted, Scott relented and Odd13 brewed a hazy IPA. Codename: Superfan was an almost immediate success, one that changed the course of the brewery and the brewing scene in the county.[41] In 2015, Odd13 brewed eleven hundred barrels of beer.

Half a mile south, the Post Brewing Co. opened at the beginning of 2014, just five months behind Odd13, inside the former Veterans of Foreign Wars Post 1771.

The Post was the brainchild of the Big Red F Restaurant Group—a handful of restaurants under the watchful eye of chef Dave Query. Formed in 1994, the Big Red F had always wanted to open a brewery, but to open a brewery in Colorado, you had to be "holy-shit good," Cherice Engel told *Boulder Weekly* in 2014. That moment came when the Post managed to lure brewmaster Bryan Selders back to the brewing game. Selders, who had previously brewed for Delaware's Dogfish Head Brewing, left the industry in 2011 to pursue web design. It didn't stick, and in 2013, Selders relocated to Lafayette and started building Big Red F's first brewery.

Slinging hot chicken and cold beer, the Post quickly found its legs, and Selders won a silver medal for the flagship pilsner, Howdy Beer, in 2014 and a gold in 2016 for Achtertuin Seizoen (Dutch for "backyard season") Farmhouse Ale.

Much in the same way brewing called Selders back from the software world, Dogfish Head beckoned Selders back from Colorado. In 2017, Selders left the Post to rejoin Dogfish Head as its brewing ambassador. But the Post concept proved durable, and the Big Red F opened a restaurant-only component in Longmont in early 2016 and another brewery in Boulder, at the storied 2027 Thirteenth Street location, in late 2017.

Davin Helden, Eric Briggs and Seth Townsend closed out Lafayette's brewery boom, opening Liquid Mechanics Brewing Company in August 2014—a little more than twelve months after Front Range became the first. It took Boulder almost a decade to get to four breweries; Longmont took two. Lafayette did it in a year.

EPILOGUE

And with the right kind of eyes you can almost see the high-water mark—that place where the wave finally broke and rolled back.
—Hunter S. Thompson, Fear and Loathing in Las Vegas

Boulder County added three new breweries in 2015 (Longmont's Skeye Brewing Company and Wibby Brewing, and Boulder's Vision Quest Brewing Company), and Avery Brewing Co. moved to its state-of-the-art facility in Gunbarrel.

Across the country, 620 breweries opened, bringing the total number to 4,847. It was the highest number of operating breweries in the United States since 1873, when they numbered 4,131.

That same year, the Brewers Association reported that craft beer's volume exports surpassed $116 million. The nations that inspired David Hummer to start all-grain homebrewing, that planted the seed of the Great American Beer Festival in Charlie Papazian's brain, that encouraged Adam Avery to explore wild fermentation, that spurred Eric Wallace to make beer that didn't suck were returning the favor and importing beer to the tune of 400,000 barrels a year.

Then there were the losses. On March 6, 2015, Otto Zavatone, Boulder Brewing Company's first brewmaster, died at the age of seventy-four. A year later, David Hummer, cofounder of the same brewery, passed away on December 17, 2016. He was eighty-two.

In January of that year, Papazian, the most influential noncommercial brewer in the movement, stepped down as president of the Brewers Association, handing the reins over to Bob Pease.[42] In May, Twisted Pine Brewing Company pulled distribution and cut production in half to focus on the taproom. And in November, Avery discontinued seven of its legacy ales: the Beast, Samael's, Mephistopheles, the Kaiser, the Czar, Salvation and duganA.

Boulder County beer was changing.

WHY BOULDER?

This book began with a simple question: Why Boulder? Why are the Brewers Association and the American Homebrewers Association headquartered here? Why did Charlie Papazian, Eric Wallace, Adam Avery, Matt Cutter, Dale Katechis, David Zuckerman, Kevin Daly, Tom Horst, George Hanna and on and on and on and on come here, set up shop here, build an industry here? Why was the first craft brewery in Colorado—now known as the "State of Craft Beer" and the "Napa Valley of Beer"—named Boulder Brewing when it wasn't even located in Boulder? Hummer and Ware's license listed Longmont in the address box, and the physical brewery was in Hygiene. Why Boulder Beer?

"I liked that name; it was right on target," Ware said in 2019. "And it says it like it is. It tells you what's going on: it's bolder, and it's beer."

It wasn't much more complicated than that. "When we started at the goat shed, we had no idea of starting a business," Ware said. "It was, 'Hey, we want to brew beer.' And then in order to brew beer, we found out we got to get a license, we gotta do this, we gotta do that. All the rest of it."

Ware's "all the rest of it" morphed from a single business into an entire industry of producers and consumers.

Jeff Brown, former president of Boulder Beer, said, "Everything from the manufacturing of wearables to books being written to hop farmers in Paonia, who, twenty years ago, never would have thought about growing hops. And here they are, supplying local products to local breweries."

Papazian: "The marketing people and the packaging people and PR people and the tour buses—the tour buses have to buy vehicles and hire people to maintain them."

Wallace: "It's kind of a bigger trend that we didn't fall into; we helped create it."

Avery: "Beer is just a part of this artisanal movement, and now it's moved all the way from just artisanal to location, and that local kind of feeling."

Craft brewers instilled value in beer, rescuing it from the bottom shelf and elevating it into something worthy of a culture, an economy and a way of life.

"I never did imagine, could imagine, the impact," Papazian said.

AFTER THE END

History never ends when it's convenient. It just goes. Stories, on the other hand, end by design. And, with that in mind, the story of *Boulder County Beer* comes to its end in 2015. To borrow a line from Orson Welles: Every story has a happy ending—if you know where to stop.

I started putting this book together in summer 2019, with most of the writing done in the spring of 2020. Both, for reasons we'll get into in a minute, seem like perfectly good places to stop. Maybe they are better ones. After all, Boulder Beer Co. celebrated its fortieth anniversary on July 20, 2019—the first craft brewery in the country to do so. That summer, brewmaster David Zuckerman handed over the brew spoon to Rob Black, who joined the company in 2012, and the future looked bright—at least it did in July. Three months later, the brewery announced it would cease distribution altogether, scaling back production from sixteen thousand barrels a year to maybe one thousand, and focus on the brewpub on Wilderness Place. Then, on January 6, 2020, president Gina Day announced that the brewery would close, and the building on Wilderness Place would be sold. The brand would live on with the six core beers being brewed and distributed by a contract brewery in Denver, Sleeping Giant Brewing Company, but the brewery as so many knew it through forty years would close on January 18, 2020.

It was a tough week for Boulder. Wild Woods Brewing Company closed its doors on January 11, and now the oldest brewery in the county was doing the same. The atmosphere in the Pub on Wilderness that day was elegiac. Many gathered for one last pint, but no one seemed shocked that Boulder Beer would soon be no more. Saddened, yes, but not shocked. Most had taken the brand for granted for years. Even die-hard beer enthusiasts had forgotten the roots, distracted—or enticed—by the "what's next monster," as Zuckerman put it. I interviewed Zuckerman in the summer of 2019 inside Boulder Beer's conference room, the shelves cluttered with dusty bottles and cans of beers past and present. Built in the early 1980s, the building reflected it. Established in 1979, the brand felt it. Twelve hundred miles to the west, California's Sierra Nevada Brewing Company, which passed the fortieth milestone in 2020, was doing better than ever. Its iconic Pale Ale somehow never fell out of favor with the times. Boulder Beer had many flagships—Buffalo Gold, Hazed & Infused, Shake Chocolate Porter—but none cracked the production level or critical regard of Sierra Nevada's Pale. First in Colorado and first in Boulder was the brewery's greatest asset, but it wasn't enough. The brewing scene had moved on.

The scene had also moved on from Walnut Brewery. It poured its last pint on June 4, 2017. One month later, the brewpub reopened as a Boulder Beer outpost. Brewer Rodney Taylor stayed on, as did most of the waitstaff, but it wasn't the same. Boulder Beer on Walnut closed in summer 2018 and reopened again as Squared Pizza + Beer (still owned by the Days). The third time wasn't a charm, and the brewpub finally closed in December 2018.

It was a tough couple of years for the Days. In January 2017, the original Old Chicago Pizza and Taphouse on Pearl Street closed, and the building was torn down on April 1, 2020. Earlier that March, Craftworks—the company that now owned Old Chicago and Rock Bottom, among others—filed for Chapter 11 bankruptcy protection. On March 31, 2020, the company laid off all eighteen thousand employees.

Breweries were opening in triplicate, but the scene was showing its age. In 2018, the Great American Beer Festival welcomed sixty-two thousand guests—its highest attendance at that point—but lost something along the way.[43] A few of the brewers I spoke with decried the festival's ties with Jameson Whiskey, which sponsored a large arena and partnered with a handful of breweries, and the sports-bar chain Buffalo Wild Wings. It was an odd moment, for sure, to enter a cordoned-off section of the convention hall to eat chicken wings in front of TV screens playing college football. At one point, the game cut to a Bud Light commercial that was mocking drinkers with flavor preferences. "Bud Light," the commercial concluded, "for the many, not the few."

But not many at the Buffalo Wild Wings pavilion heard the commercial's tag over the din of the crowds drinking, discussing and cheering beers. The irony cut both ways.

BY THE END OF 2015, forty-two breweries were operating in the county, and eighteen more would join their ranks by the end of the decade.[44] The majority of these breweries would rely on the taproom experience. With a constantly rotating selection of seasonals, one-offs and pilot batches, breweries would shift gear from flagships and packaging to variety and experimentation. Food trucks partnered with breweries, a different one each night. Patrons could ostensibly visit the same brewery and drink a different beer and have a different meal each night of the week.

Not all survived.[45] But if there was any sign that the market was maturing, it was the impressive uptick in openings and closures—with the former outpacing the latter. In April 2020, Bart Watson, chief economist for the Brewers Association, referred to these five years as the "At the Brewery Era": "A unique moment in brewing history."

A unique moment that came to an abrupt halt on March 16, 2020.

BREWING IN THE TIME OF CORONAVIRUS

On March 16, 2020, at the advice of health officials, Colorado governor Jared Polis ordered the closure of all dine-in service at restaurants, bars, breweries, brewpubs and taprooms in an attempt to slow the spread of COVID-19. Breweries, brewpubs and taprooms could still sell beer; they just couldn't allow people inside to drink it. Sales fell off a cliff, and owners scrambled to pivot their business models from in-store sales to pick-up and delivery.

For more than two months, every brewery in the county closed its doors in some capacity. Though the bulk of research done for this book preceded the pandemic, most of the writing and editing happened during and immediately following the shutdown. As I write these words in June 2020, no brewery in Boulder County has closed up shop for good, but none of them are doing well. The bigger breweries with larger distribution footprints and deeper pockets at least appear to be doing better than the rest, but looks can be deceiving.

History takes time to unfold, and the nuances and effects of the coronavirus pandemic on the brewing industry won't present themselves for years to come. Hell, the greater implications of the At the Brewery Era won't present themselves for at least a couple more years. It took over a decade for brewers and restaurateurs to see what Boulder Brewing was up to and decide to join in on the fun. It took another decade to establish viable supply chains and market access and yet another to make the business an attractive enterprise.

To borrow a thought from Papazian, it would be wrong to call Hummer and Ware pioneers in the brewing industry. They were the explorers without a map. The pioneers followed them—the first brewpub and the first taproom, the first to put their beer in a can and the first to barrel age it. Then came the settlers, the ones who set up shop in between and connected the dots. They transformed a dozen breweries scattered around the county into a community—from a hobby gone berserk to an industry representing thousands.

"It's bolder, and it's beer."

ONE LAST GOODBYE

Pick up any book on the history of the craft beer revolution, and you'll read of waves—first wave brewers, second wave brewers, third wave and so on. These demarcations are nonsense, more or less, change from author to author and don't adhere to any strict chronology.

But the metaphor seems apt, even if Boulder is a landlocked county without a beach in sight. When I spoke to Wallace in the winter of 2019, he used the word *tsunami* to describe how the craft beer revolution coincided with café culture, slow foods and other artisanal/craft movements.

And like waves crashing on a shore, some are bigger than others. Some take longer to build. Some come in quick succession, inching their way up the sand on the backs of their predecessors. Some draw deep breaths, leeching the water from the sand as they pull back and gather for a mighty crash.

But the waves keep coming. Still or choppy, high tide or low, they lap endlessly at the shore. This book has covered the first big wave of beer in Boulder County and the little waves that followed. Today, the sea is rolling back out, gathering itself and taking everything with it. But tomorrow, the water will return, and it will crash again. There will be a second wave. And then a third, and then a fourth and so on.

It's inevitable.

NOTES

Part I

1. Established as Boulder Brewing Company in 1979, the company changed name three times throughout the years: Boulder Beer Company (1990–93), Rockies Brewing Company (1993–2005) and Boulder Beer Co. (2005–20). All four names are used throughout the book and coincide with either the time period discussed or to signal the era in which an interviewee worked at the brewery.
2. This process is known as lautering, where the husks of the malt form a filter bed that separates the solids from the sweet wort (water infused with the sugary starches from the malted grains).
3. By contrast, Julius Hummer described Ware's homebrewing technique as "hippyish," fitting for the city he lived in. "Honey and wild hops as I recall."
4. Naturally conditioned, yeast-in-the-bottle packaging involves dosing still (uncarbonated) beer with yeast and a small amount of sugar. When yeast consumes sugar, it produces carbon dioxide, which, if the beer is sealed, will carbonate the beer. Done correctly, a naturally conditioned beer is a thing of beauty. But too much or too little can cause a variety of flaws, and when combined with lactobacillus, the yeast can produce too much carbonation, turning a glass bottle of beer into a ticking time bomb.
5. A catch-all term to refer to small breweries, *microbrewery* was first coined by *Zymurgy* news editor Stuart Harris in the early 1980s. In 1984, Vince Cottone—a writer based in Seattle—began using the term *craft brewery*

to describe similar breweries. As the years progressed, *craft* replaced *micro* in both newspaper coverage and marketing, and I favor its use in the book (using the word *craft* ninety-six times, as opposed to the twenty-one times *micro* appears in this text). Note: The definition of *craft* has also undergone a few iterations throughout the years, particularly in regard to ownership of a brewery. Most of the breweries in this book meet the Brewers Association's definition as a craft brewery. Some do not. But at one time or another, they were all craft breweries, hence my liberal use of the word throughout.

6. Designed to mimic European breweries and Scottish distilleries, Boulder Brewing prominently displayed the brewhouse—complete with copper kettle and mash tun—topped by a tall cupola. On brew days, steam would billow out of the double triangles of the cupola.
7. Thirty years later, pioneered by a handful of New England–based breweries, hazy, unfiltered ales would become all the rage. Boulder Beer would try to keep pace with Due East, a New England–style IPA, but would fail to capitalize on the fad.
8. When the Greenlees bought Boulder Brewing with the Days, Bob was a Boulder city councilman (he served from 1983 to 1999). In 1998, Greenlee was elected mayor of Boulder; he would serve for one year.
9. Lebesch and partner Kim Jordan started Fort Collins's New Belgium Brewery in their basement in 1991 on a small, handmade seven-barrel system. Their second batch of beer, a Belgian-style amber ale named Fat Tire, changed the landscape of craft brewing and became one of the most successful beers in the movement. Two years later, the couple had to expand, so Lebesch placed an ad for his used equipment.
10. Paul Gatza started homebrewing in 1990, worked on Boulder Beer's bottling line and worked and owned two homebrew supply shops in the Boulder area. In 1998, Gatza started working for the Boulder-based Association of Brewers (AOB)—later renamed the Brewers Association when the AOB merged with the Brewers Association of America in 2005—and the American Homebrewers Association, eventually working his way up to senior vice president of professional brewing division at the Brewers Association. In 2014, Baile paid homage to Gatza by releasing a gratzer—a Polish-style smoke beer—aptly named Paul Gratzer.
11. Named after his chocolate lab, Elle's Brown Ale became Ellie's Brown Ale after *Elle* magazine issued a cease and desist letter.
12. Brewer Vinnie Cilurzo of Temecula, California's Blind Pig Brewery is credited with brewing the first double IPA—or imperial IPA, depending

on whom you talk to—in 1994. A few others followed, notably Stone Brewing in 1998 with its Second Anniversary IPA.

13. In 2006, Arthur opened his own brewery, the Lost Abbey.
14. Salvation brought Avery in collaboration with Cilurzo, now located at Russian River Brewing Company in Santa Rosa, California. Both were producing a Belgian-style ale with the same name, and rather than litigate over ownership, the two blended their beers for Collaboration Not Litigation, a Belgian-style strong ale.
15. Billy Phillips was one of the brewers at the Oasis Annex and joined Twisted Pine as the warehouse manager when Bob Baile moved Twisted Pine into the Annex. "We used to joke that when we unlocked the doors after a year of vacancy, Billy was still in the building," Baile said.
16. Even the Oasis Brewers Pub on Canyon Boulevard wasn't vacant long. Republic of Boulder moved in August 2004 but closed in April 2006.
17. A lot of brewers in the county got around, and Lutz and Watson were no exception. They might also hold the record for fewest beers produced by a brewery: one. In 2006, the two brewed and packaged a Belgian quadrupel while working at Left Hand under the name WoodVille Brewing Co.
18. The name Upslope is derived from a Front Range weather pattern. In short, warm, moist air from the Gulf of Mexico clashes with cold air descending from the northwest. The heavy, wet air is forced up the slope of the Rocky Mountains, dumping precipitation in the process, often in the form of snow—the same white gold that called Cutter to Colorado in the first place.
19. Trappist beer is brewed at breweries located in the walls of Trappist abbeys and brewed by Trappist monks—the name originates from La Trappe Abbey in Normandy, France, founded in 1664. Beers brewed outside Trappist walls cannot be labeled as such and frequently incur the litigious wrath of Belgian monks protecting their trademark. When Lutz first brewed the ale, it resulted in a cease and desist letter. Lutz relented and renamed the beer Angry Monk.
20. Most beer is fermented with *Saccharomyces cerevisiae*, also known as ale yeast, or *Saccharomyces pastorianus*, also known as lager yeast. A fair number of European breweries have relied on various classifications of Brettanomyces yeast, or Brett, to further develop funky, wild and sour flavors in the finished beer.
21. In April 2008, Avery bottled Fifteen, its anniversary ale fermented with 100 percent Brettanomyces yeast culled from Drie Fonteinen. According to Andy Parker, Boulder drinkers had no idea what to do with the beer,

and the brewery ended up sitting on kegs of Fifteen for months. A decade later, a handful of breweries in the county were not only experimenting with Brett fermentation but also devoting entire breweries to the yeast.

Part II

22. In January 2012, the Brewers Association Board of Directors and staff convened at the Kitchen in Boulder to record an audio history of the craft brewing industry. At the event, Wallace told a different account of hiring Lutz: Wallace was delivering kegs to La Estrellita when Lutz asked him if Left Hand was hiring. "You want to do this?" Wallace asked, gesturing to the kegs. "If you want to do this, I'm hiring." Lutz went to Left Hand the following day and became the brewery's fourth employee.
23. Following the repeal of Prohibition, Colorado liquor law limited licenses to one license per retail liquor store, effectively making every liquor store in Colorado independent and allowing brewery owners the ability to negotiate one-on-one with store owners. This access to market was indispensable to small breweries and became a significant factor in fostering Colorado's craft beer market. In 2016, Senate Bill 16-197 was signed into law and changed liquor licensing in the state. As of 2019, retail liquor stores could hold multiple licenses.
24. Dennis Coombs became the mayor of Longmont (2011–17), joining a number of Colorado politicians who got their start in the brewing world.
25. Like many stories, the name behind Oskar Blues has multiple points of origin. Brewer Dave Chichura (2005–13) liked to spin a tale of Katechis (sometimes Katechis's mother) coming across an unfilmed script of *The Blues Brothers* at a garage sale. In the script, a third brother, Oskar, joined Jake and Elwood Blues. To quote beer writer Cat Wolinski, "This is entirely untrue."
26. According to Katechis, canning beer was not warmly received in-house. Lutz "was a purist," Katechis said. "And trying to get him to put his beer, our beer, in a can was laughable."
27. Both Sierra Nevada Brewing Company and New Belgium Brewing announced North Carolina production facilities before Oskar Blues (Mills River and Asheville, respectively), but Oskar Blues beat both to the finish line. Sierra Nevada cut the ribbon on its Mills River facility on March 10, 2015, and New Belgium followed on May 2, 2016.

28. In homebrew parlance, a clone is a homemade replica of a commercial beer—often a popular one. Since most commercial brewers were once homebrewers, clones are a time-honored tradition with the professional publishing recipes aimed at amateurs looking to emulate classic styles with readily available ingredients.
29. Tom Boogaard, a former brewer and sales manager at Avery Brewing, founded Wild Mountain Smokehouse & Brewery with his wife, Cori, in 2006.
30. Founded in 1883, VLB Berlin (*Versuchs- und Lehranstalt für Brauerei in Berlin e. V.*) is a renowned brewing education institution focusing on academic and practical execution of brewing knowledge. The Certified Brewmaster Course dates to 1999.

Part III

31. As the story goes, Dave and Jan Robertson were picking up their son from a Maine summer camp when they told Papazian to drop by if he ever found himself in Boulder. Not long after, Papazian darkened their door and set roots in the Centennial State.
32. In 1984, Avon/HarperCollins published the first edition with the new title, *The Complete Joy of Homebrewing*.
33. As Dave Robertson recounted in a 2003 issue of *Zymurgy*, "[Papazian] ran a marble tournament, and there was a pie contest. He has all sorts of activities. He was, and has continued to be, a magnet."
34. Headquartered in Pottsville, Pennsylvania, and founded in 1829, D.G. Yuengling & Sons is the oldest operating brewery in the United States. Located in New Ulm, Minnesota, and founded in 1860, August Schell Brewing Company is the second-oldest brewery in the United States. The Anchor Brewing Company was founded in San Francisco in 1896 but fell into disrepair and almost closed for good until Frederick Louis "Fritz" Maytag III bought the brewery in 1965 and saved it from obliteration. Many consider this moment to be the beginning of the American craft beer revolution.
35. The categories that year: ales, alts, American cream ales, American lagers, American light lagers, bocks/doppelbocks, continental pilsners, porters, stouts, Vienna-style lagers and wheat beers.
36. Originating from Köln (Cologne), Germany, circa 874, kölsch is light, easy-drinking ale with a flavor profile closer to a Bavarian lager than

American pale ale. Featuring subdued hop characteristics, smooth malt and fruity esters, thanks to top-fermenting yeast, kölsch caught on with American brewers and drinkers in the 2010s the way amber ale had in the 1990s.

37. In 2010, Rock Bottom, which included Walnut Brewery and Old Chicago Pizza & Tap House, merged with the Gordon Biersch Brewing Company, another brewpub chain, to create CraftWorks Holding. The company was headquartered in Nashville, Tennessee, with an additional restaurant support office in Denver.

38. Brewers express gravity in two terms: original gravity, which measures the content of solids in the wort before fermentation, and final gravity, which measures the density of the beer to the density of the water following fermentation. The former is used to determine the content of sugar in the wort, and the latter is used to determine the conversion of sugar to alcohol in the finished beer.

39. Another brewing term, 12Degrees is a reference to the Plato gravity scale, which measures the concentration of dissolved solids (alcohol) in the wort. This scale, which is used commonly on Belgian brewed ales, is expressed in degrees Plato (°P), with each 1°P representing 0.4 percent. 12°P, by the way, translates to a 5.0 percent alcohol by volume beer.

40. John Kimmich first brewed Heady Topper—an unfiltered, unpasteurized double IPA—in January 2004. Over the following decade, the beer developed a cult following.

41. Using late hop additions, a grain bill that looked beyond two-row pale malt and different yeast strains, Odd13 set the standard for hop-saturated IPAs in Boulder County. These beers favored aroma over bitterness, fleshy fruit over citrus rind and tropical sweetness over piney and resinous snap.

Epilogue

42. Papazian fully retired from the Brewers Association on January 23, 2019, his seventieth birthday. Later that year, Papazian was asked why he never started a brewery. With a twinkle in his eye and a soft-spoken demeanor, he replied, "I've thought a lot about opening a brewery. I've thought about it, and thought about it, and thought about it, and thought a lot about it, which is why I never opened one."

43. The stats for the 2018 Great American Beer Festival are staggering: 62,000 attendees and 800 breweries pouring 4,000 beers. The competition

featured 102 categories (plus Pro-Am and collaboration) with 8,496 beers from 2,404 breweries. How did they pull it off? With 4,393 volunteers donating nearly seventy thousand hours.

44. In 2016, Nederland's Wild Mountain Smokehouse & Brewery closed, and James Peak Brewery & Smokehouse opened in its place; Kettle and Spoke Brewery opened in Boulder, a stone's throw away from Vision Quest Brewing Company; and brewer Zach Nichols left Sanitas Brewing Company to open Cellar West Artisan Ales in North Boulder. In 2017, UTurn BBQ opened a brewpub in Lafayette; Bootstrap Brewing opened a second—and much larger—facility in Longmont; Open Door Brewing Company became the first brewery to call Longmont's Prospect New Town neighborhood home; Gunbarrel Brewing Company became the fifth brewery to join the northeast Boulder region; Boulder Beer took over the Walnut Brewery; Endo Brewing Company joined the Lafayette scene; The Post Brewing Co. took over the brewpub at 2027 Thirteenth Street; and Beyond the Mountain Brewing opened in Boulder near Gunbarrel. In 2018, Primitive Beer, Brewmented and Collision Brewing Company all opened in Longmont; Redgarden Restaurant and Brewery opened in Louisville; Stein Brewing Co. took over the J. Wells Brewery's Boulder digs; and Squared Pizza + Beer replaced Boulder Beer on Walnut. In 2019, Cellar West Artisan Ales relocated to Lafayette and Vision Quest's Adam Kandle opened Adamant Brewing & Blending in the North Boulder space; Knotted Root Brewing Company joined the Nederland scene; Unnamed Brewing Company opened in Boulder; Mother Tucker Brewery (headquartered in Thornton, Colorado) opened its second location in Louisville; and Busey Brews closed out the decade, opening in the old James Peak Smokehouse and Brewery.

45. In 2016, Nederland's Wild Mountain Smokehouse & Brewery sold its last pint on September 29. In 2017, Shine Restaurant and Gathering Place left 2027 Thirteenth Street, Boulder, and the brewing business. In 2018, Niwot's Powder Keg Brewing Company closed on March 10; Gunbarrel's Vindication Brewing Company followed on April 28; Longmont's Skeye Brewing Company closed on June 25, with Open Door Brewing Company shutting its doors on June 29; Boulder Beer on Walnut closed in September, with the revamped concept Squared + Pizza closing the doors for good on December 11. The year 2019 claimed four: Lafayette's UTurn BBQ on January 22, Boulder's FATE Brewing Company on May 27, Longmont's Brewmented on August 31 and James Peak Smokehouse & Brewery on October 19.

BIBLIOGRAPHY

Author Interviews

Anderson, Ashlee (Shoes & Brews), February 28, 2020.

Avery, Adam (Avery Brewing Co.), January 12, 2019.

Brown, Jeff (Boulder Beer Co.), July 1, 2019.

Coyne, Chris, and Michael Memsic (Sanitas Brewing Co.), July 18, 2019.

Daly, Kevin (Mountain Sun Pubs & Breweries), January 23, 2019.

Fiorilli, John (Mountain Sun Pubs & Breweries), January 25, 2018, and January 29, 2020.

Green, Jeffrey (Very Nice Brewing Company), December 23, 2019.

Hanna, George (Oasis Brewer Pub/Oasis Brewery Annex), January 31, 2020.

Horst, Tom (Crystal Springs Brewing Company), June 6, 2019.

Hummer, Julian (Boulder Brewing Company/Gravity Brewing Company), July 15–25, 2019.

Katechis, Dale (Oskar Blues Brewery), February 25, 2020.

Papazian, Charlie (American Homebrewers Association, Brewers Association, et al.), September 19, 2019.

Puchner, Alex (BJ's Restaurants & Brewhouse), February 11, 2020.

Wallace, Eric (Left Hand Brewing Company), January 23, 2019.

Ware, Randolph (Boulder Beer Co.), June 30, 2019.

Waugh, Kent (Overland Stage Stop Brewery), March 6, 2020.

Wibby, Ryan (Wibby Brewing), June 21, 2018.

Zuckerman, David (Boulder Beer Co.), July 22, 2019.

Interviews Conducted by Theresa McCulla

Theresa McCulla is the curator of the National Museum of American History, Smithsonian Institution's American Brewing History Initiative. Since 2017, McCulla has been collecting oral histories and artifacts from American brewers. She was gracious enough to share the following interviews with me. For more on McCulla's work, visit americanhistory.si.edu/brewing-history.

Avery, Adam; Parker, Andy; Rizzo, Fred; and Rupp, Travis (Avery Brewing Co.), May 2, 2017.

Papazian, Charlie (American Homebrewers Association, Brewers Association, et al.), May 1, 2017.

Wallace, Eric, and Doore, Dick (Left Hand Brewing Company), May 3, 2017.

Zuckerman, David (Boulder Beer Co.), May 1, 2017.

Books

Acitelli, Tom. *The Audacity of Hops: The History of America's Craft Beer Revolution*. Chicago: Chicago Review Press, 2017.

Alworth, Jeff. *The Beer Bible.* New York: Workman Publishing Co., 2015.

Frank, John. *Beer Lover's Colorado*. 2nd ed. Guilford, CT: Globe Pequot, 2019.

Hickenlooper, John, and Maximillian Potter. *The Opposite of Woe: My Life in Beer and Politics*. New York: Penguin Press, 2016.

McLeod, Robert W. *Ghost Breweries of Colorado: A History of Centennial State Brewing*. Arvada, CO: self-published, 2016.

Oliver, Garrett, ed. *The Oxford Companion to Beer*. New York: Oxford University Press, 2006.

Papazian, Charlie. *The Complete Joy of Homebrewing*. 4th ed. New York: HarperCollins, 2014.

———. *Microbrewed Adventures: A Lupulin-Filled Journey to the Heart and Flavor of the World's Great Craft Beers*. New York: HarperCollins, 2005.

Pettem, Silvia. *Only in Boulder: The County's Colorful Characters*. Charleston, SC: The History Press, 2010.

Rabin, Dan. *Colorado Breweries*. Mechanicsburg, PA: Stackpole Books, 2014.

Sealover, Ed. *Mountain Brew: A Guide to Colorado's Breweries*. Charleston, SC: The History Press, 2011.

Tierney-Jones, Adrian, ed. *1001 Beers You Must Taste Before You Die*. London: Quintessence, 2013.

Magazines

Arthur, Tomme, Adam Avery, Sam Calagione, Vinnie Cilurzo and Rob Tod. "A Pilgrimage to Belgium." *New Brewer*, September–October 2006.

"Boulder Brewing Grand Opening." *New Brewer*, July/August 1985.

Gatza, Paul. "2008 Year in Review: The Glass Is More Than Half Full." *New Brewer*, May/June 2009.

Hieronymus, Stan. "The Origins of the American Homebrewers Association." *Zymurgy*, November/December 2003.

Miller, Virginia. "Interview: Spirit Hound Distillers, Craig Engelhorn & Wayne Anderson." *Distiller*, December 1, 2018.

Shellenberger, Diana. "Brew News: A Beer for Women." *New Brewer*, January/February 2001.

Shikes, Jonathan. "From the Source: Odd13 Brewing." *Beer Advocate*, March 2017.

Truesdale, Lisa. "Lafayette's 'Saloon Row' Has Something New on Tap." *Boulder Magazine*, Summer 2019.

Newspaper and Internet Articles

Antonation, Mark. "Walrus Saloon Closes After 35 Years in Downtown Boulder." *Westword*, May 22, 2018.

Asimov, Eric. "Crisp, Complex and Refreshing." *New York Times*, June 29, 2005.

"BA Pioneers: A Narrative History." Brewers Association. January 2012. BrewersAssociation.org.

Bassett, Win. "West Flanders Brewing Opens in Old BJ's Location in September." *All About Beer*, August 30, 2012.

Brewbound staff. "New Belgium Founder Remembers Gordon Knight." Brewbound.com. February 7, 2011.

Butler, Mary. "All in the Family." *Daily Camera*, August 15, 2009.

Carol, Taylor. "Boulder County History: Boulder's Prohibition Finally Ended in 1967." *Daily Camera*, December 28, 2017.

Daily Camera. David Hummer obituary, January 3, 2016.

Gross, Josh. "D-Day at the Post Brewing Company." *Boulder Weekly*, January 9, 2014.

Heinritz, Chris. "The Sink Celebrates 25 Years of Traditions Upheld Under Heinritz Brothers Ownership." The Sink. September 20, 2017. www.thesink.com.

Meehan, Chris. "Wild Goose Canning." *Company Week*, January 26, 2015.

"Meet the Rascal—Andy Parker." *Avery Brewing Co.* (blog). February 22, 2017. Blog.averybrewing.com.

"Meet the Rascal—Larry Avery." *Avery Brewing Co.* (blog). March 30, 2017. Blog.averybrewing.com.

Meltzer, Erica. "Boulder's Kettle and Stone Brewing to Change Name to Avoid Trademark Fight." *Daily Camera*, April 11, 2014.

Otto Zavatone obituary. Dignity Memorial. March 10, 2015. Dignitymemorial.com.

"Remembering Gordon Knight." Oskar Blues Brewery. February 7, 2019. Oskarblues.com.

Shikes, Jonathan. "Avery Brewing Kills Off Six of Its Acclaimed Demons and Dictator Beers." *Westword*, November 21, 2016.

Silver, Maya. "Brewery Snapshot: West Flanders Brewing Co." *Dining Out Denver & Boulder*.

"Summary: H.R.1337—95th Congress (1977–1978)." Congress.gov.

Summit Daily. Harriett Bobo obituary, July 25, 2018.

Wallace, Alicia. "The Kettle & Stone Brewing Opening This Week in Gunbarrel." *Daily Camera*, June 23, 2013.

Wolinski, Cat. "12 Things You Should Know About Oskar Blues Brewery." VinePair. October 5, 2018. VinePair.com.

INDEX

S

T

U

V

W

Y

Z

ABOUT THE AUTHOR

Since 2016, Michael Casey has covered beer and brewing for *Boulder Weekly*, the city's last independently owned print newspaper. He also writes about movies and lives in Lakewood with his wife, Lindsay; cat, Vivian; and several philodendrons. This is his first book.